HIGH
AND
TIGHT

VILLARD

NEW YORK

THE RISE AND FALL OF

DWIGHT GOODEN

AND

DARRYL STRAWBERRY

HIGH AND TIGHT

BOB KLAPISCH

Copyright © 1996 by Bob Klapisch

All rights reserved under International and Pan-American Copyright
Conventions. Published in the United States by Villard Books, a divi-
sion of Random House, Inc., New York, and simultaneously in
Canada by Random House of Canada Limited, Toronto.

Villard Books is a registered trademark of Random House, Inc.

Library of Congress Cataloging-in-Publication Data
Klapisch, Bob.
High and tight : the rise and fall of Dwight Gooden and Darryl
Strawberry / by Bob Klapisch.
p.   cm.
ISBN 0-679-44899-3
1. Gooden, Dwight.   2. Strawberry, Darryl.   3. Baseball players—
United States—Biography.   4. Baseball players—Drug use—United
States.   I. Title.
GV865.G62K53   1996
796.357'092'2—dc20
[B]   96-10532

Printed in the United States of America on acid-free paper
10 9 8 7 6 5 4 3 2 1
First Edition
Book design by Jo Anne Metsch

For Jacques Klapisch.
My first coach, my best friend.

ACKNOWLEDGMENTS

This book would not have been possible without the help and inspiration of several people. I would like to thank David Rosenthal, my editor at Villard, along with Amy Edelman and Jennifer Webb, for their literary and technical support; my agent, David Vigliano, for finding a home for the project; my colleagues Mark Kriegel, John Giannone, and Dave Kaplan for helping conceptualize and research it. I would also like to recognize Tom Verducci of *Sports Illustrated*, whose February 27, 1995, cover story helped inspire this book.

Finally, my gratitude to those who helped keep me strong: Stephanie "Lil Moose" Stokes; James Jones; John House; Steven Gustavson; my attorney, Peter Johnson, Jr.; and my godson, Ricky DeNiro.

And, obviously, I would like to acknowledge Darryl Strawberry and Dwight Gooden—who provided scenes from a self-written script about his life. Their willingness to lower the walls of their past and relive many painful moments made this book a reality.

B.K.

January 1996

CONTENTS

INTRODUCTION

NO SPORTS TRAGEDY so deeply touched the hearts of Americans as that of Mickey Mantle, who stood naked before a country and, as a recovering alcoholic, asked that children not look up to him. "Please, don't live your life the way I did," Mantle said, perhaps not grasping that, in his final message, he had finally lived up to his "responsibility" as an athletic hero.

But it took most of Mantle's life—indeed, his entire playing career—to understand the value of redemption. Before being admitted to the Betty Ford Clinic in 1994, the Mick's days were a nonstop blur of home runs and stiff drinks. By the time he stopped abusing his body, Mantle realized it was too late to undo his mistakes. Being a poor father, Mantle said, made him weep until the day he died.

Of course, Mantle was no different from all too many public figures. From Jimi Hendrix to Liza Minnelli, from Len Bias to Anthony Hopkins, the newspapers are filled with tales of addiction and, sometimes, recovery. It's practically an iron equation that with fame comes wealth, which evolves into temptation. Some survive the inevitable dance with alcohol, drugs, and women; many do not.

When Dwight Gooden and Darryl Strawberry first arrived at Shea Stadium in the mid-eighties, they were immediately raised to the level of deities, the hippest of the hip, the reason to watch the Mets. Of course, no one bothered to ask Doc and Darryl, aged just nineteen and twenty-one, if they were ready for the coronation; the crown was simply handed to them. Overnight, their bank accounts were swollen beyond all dreams and so was their recognition factor. Magazines competed to put Gooden and Strawberry on their covers, and reporters spent hours at their lockers, waiting for the one exclusive quote that could make for a back-page headline.

It wasn't just the press that clustered. Everywhere Gooden and Strawberry went, there were fans who offered drinks, women who offered dates, or those special "friends" who made sure to offer a line of cocaine in the bathroom of a nightclub. Dwight and Darryl certainly weren't the only Mets who experimented with drugs in the eighties. They just happened to fall the farthest.

In a sense, the two were easy prey: Gooden and Strawberry were the youngest Mets, the team's only black superstars, and, because they were blessed with such talent, perhaps the most naïve. These were two players who never had to rely on hard work to succeed and never grasped how fleeting physical skill can be. Ironically, it was addiction that made Gooden and Strawberry appreciate how much they have thrown away.

This is a story about the rise and fall of two young stars whose self-discipline was no match for the fast New York

lifestyle in the eighties. It could be the story of River Phoenix
or Kurt Cobain—all of them painting the same illustration of
human failure. But it is also about recovery. Neither player
has used drugs in over a year, they claim, as they attempt to
renew their careers.

Once, they owned the future. Today, Strawberry's and
Gooden's only stake is to the next twenty-four hours, which
they pray will keep them sober.

HIGH
AND
TIGHT

1

THE RUSH

THE TACHOMETER WAS pushing close to five thousand rpm's, nowhere near red-line for a BMW 850, but the slightest vibration could be felt in the steering wheel. The engine was breathing loud, full of urgency, as the car tore through the night. One hundred miles per hour wasn't enough, though, as it failed to satisfy the beast beneath the hood and the demons within the driver. At 105, and then 110, the asphalt seemed to liquefy under the tires, which were on a straight path to nowhere.

Inside, two hands gripped the steering wheel, partially in fear, mostly in self-loathing. Dwight Gooden kept swallowing hard, his gums numb, his mind racing faster than his car's engine. The cocaine, invited into his body hours ago as a friend, now controlled him. Why can't I quit? Gooden asked himself. Why am I high again? Will it ever end?

In the fall of 1994, Gooden was deeply addicted to cocaine, suspended from baseball, routinely failing his drug tests. Despite a lengthy stay at the prestigious Betty Ford Clinic, Gooden found he was still unable to resist the pull that Tampa had over him at night, powerless to stop the BMW from heading over the Howard Frankland Bridge, which linked St. Petersburg to his old neighborhood in Tampa. He would go there. He would get high. And when it was over, Gooden would return to his BMW and drive it as fast as he could to St. Petersburg, purging himself.

If the speed didn't satisfy him by the time he'd completed his twenty-two-mile journey on Interstate 275, he would turn around and send the engine screaming back to Tampa. From there, he would begin the trek again and take the car as fast as either he or the 322 horses within it could tolerate. Only rarely were there cops around. Most of the time Gooden had the highway to himself. It was just him and an enemy that wouldn't let go.

Gooden knew that, at that speed, he would have died instantly in any accident. A pothole, a tire blowout, any road debris at all would have killed the youngest Cy Young Award winner in baseball history. Those thoughts would occur to Gooden only the next day, only after his heart had stopped sprinting and the cocaine had finally metabolized. He would make the same promises over again, to stay away from cocaine, stay out of Tampa, stay away from the BMW's red-line. Those were easy promises to make—the next day.

But now, tears streaming down his cheeks, Gooden wanted to drive the addiction out of him with the speed of his BMW. If either the car or the coke killed him first . . . well, Gooden thought, would it really matter?

THE REUNION

IT WAS JULY 1995, and, as always, the approach to the Howard Frankland Bridge was under construction. The massive BMW was forced to chug along at an insulting fifteen mph, and at that speed, other motorists on their way to Tampa could identify the driver in the Beamer. It was Dwight Gooden.

In any other year, Doc's mere presence on the highway would turn heads, raise eyebrows. He was, after all, the National League's greatest pitcher of the eighties—a presence so dominant that, as a Met, he only needed one name. Doc. From Dwight Gooden, the rookie in 1984 with the explosive fastball, he became Dr. K, the strike-out machine and then, finally, Doc, a symbol of Met superiority. But in 1995, he was back to being Dwight Gooden again and had returned to his life as a local.

Actually, it wasn't unusual for St. Petersburg residents to see Gooden around town—driving on the Frankland

Bridge, shopping at the malls, or working out in the weight room at Eckerd College. Gooden was everywhere, with plenty of time to kill. For the first summer since high school, he wasn't playing baseball but was serving a one-year suspension for violating his drug aftercare program. That was major-league baseball's sanitized explanation for Gooden's problem. He had a more candid description for his condition: "I'd become a junkie."

The reason he wasn't pitching was that in the fall of 1994, he failed at least eight drug tests. Eight times, traces of cocaine were found in his urine, living proof that the addiction that had taken him down in 1987 was still there and might indeed haunt him for the rest of his life. Gooden was already serving a sixty-day suspension for failing a June test. Now, after being released from the Betty Ford Clinic that summer, his drug use resumed, heavier than ever. "I was at the bottom, really, just about the point where I was going to throw not just my career away, but my life, too," Gooden said. Baseball was done with him, at least for 1995, maybe longer.

How could his fall have been so precipitous, so devastating? How had the cocaine put its hooks into him so deeply? Gooden had asked himself that very question so many times over the years, and there were days the despair was so deep he broke down and cried. On this day in mid-July 1995, Gooden was once again reminded of his career detour. He was driving across that Howard Frankland Bridge to meet up with a former teammate and old friend, Darryl Strawberry.

Darryl and Doc. Doc and Darryl. The two had been linked since 1984, Gooden's first year, just as the Mets were beginning their run as New York's most potent team. Gooden threw the fastballs, Strawberry hit them to the planets, and, between them, nothing could block the slick, unfettered road to Cooperstown.

They had both won Rookie of the Year awards, Strawberry in 1983, Doc a year later. Strawberry had an enormous looping swing, vulnerable to outside-corner fastballs, especially up in the zone. But try to challenge him low, and he was dangerous. In just his first year, Strawberry hit twenty-six homers, beginning a streak of hitting at least twenty-five in each of the next nine seasons. In his first five summers, Strawberry had more home runs than Mickey Mantle had in his first five. Darryl had the swing, the ego, the can't-miss name, and he was sure playing in the right city.

But so much went wrong. Suspicions of drug use started around the time Gooden went down in 1987. Although Darryl repeatedly told reporters he wasn't using cocaine, years later he confessed that the wild lifestyle the Mets led in the eighties had indeed infected him, too. There was cocaine, an addiction built upon a foundation of alcohol and amphetamines. Actually, there was cocaine everywhere in the Met clubhouse. Both Gooden and Strawberry estimated that among the twenty-five Met players, there were at least twelve who were involved with drugs. "Definitely, I'd say half the team," Strawberry said.

At the core of it were the amphetamines, which allowed the Mets to exist in an artificial reality on the ball field—to be more intense than the nondrugged player, more energetic, quicker-reflexed. The use of amphetamines was, in fact, a form of cheating, but the inner-circle Mets had created a culture where the rules either didn't exist or else were ignored. It was part of their macho credo to get as drunk or as high as possible the night before, to chase the prettiest women, and then to return to the playing field the next day and win by the biggest margin. Without amphetamines, that lifestyle could not have been sustained.

Strawberry said, "There were days I wouldn't have been able to go on the field. I was just too hung over. I never played drunk. But I played a lot of games feeling terrible." Strawberry still wonders what the alcohol and, later, cocaine did to his career. "Man, I lost years," he said wistfully.

In the eighties, though, no one worried about the future: there was too much to be had in the present. Wherever the Mets went, there were not only games to win but bars to frequent, women to meet, excesses to be indulged everywhere. The Mets of the eighties were an unmistakable group: a reporter could feel their energy the moment he or she stepped into the clubhouse. There was first baseman Keith Hernandez, the dark, brooding, tough-guy leader, the spiritual backbone in the room and point man for the media. Pitcher Ron Darling, who despite his Yale background was at the core of the Mets' inner circle. Outfielder Lenny Dykstra was the hard little leadoff hitter; at second base was the equally Napoleonic Wally Backman, his side man. Kevin Elster was the soft-hands shortstop with the movie-star looks, Davey Johnson the renegade manager, in the middle of a seven-year war with his boss, Frank Cashen, which ultimately led to his dismissal in 1991.

The Mets of the eighties were a symbol of Reagan's America: they lived hard, partied enormously, made and spent money lavishly. The Mets were to New York in the eighties as the Knicks became in the mid-nineties, hip, back-page-important, the destination in every conversational road among sports fans. It wasn't just Doc who existed on a first-name basis with fans. There was Straw, Lenny, Mex, Wally. Only rotisserie-league geeks used their full names.

Within this citywide love affair, though, there was a special attachment to Strawberry and Gooden; they were, after all, the only two black stars on an otherwise all-white team. Mookie Wilson was adored by fans, but it was Strawberry and Gooden who evoked the deepest passion from New Yorkers. Darryl was moody, difficult, boastful, misunderstood. The way he played ball represented that bipolar personality: he seemed either to crush a fastball 450 feet or else look bad striking out. From at-bat to at-bat, who could tell which Darryl would be standing at the plate?

Dwight was kinder, gentler, the product of a more stable background. Everyone liked Doc. He was more marketable, easier for the Mets to promote. There were never any spring-training explosions, like the one in 1989 when Strawberry and Hernandez punched each other out in full view of TV cameras. Gooden never walked out of camp, demanding more money. He never boasted of a "monster year" as Darryl so often did. Yet, as different as they were, they were still linked: Doc and Darryl, the two reasons for hope at Shea— not just in the eighties but, the Mets hoped, deep into the nineties, too.

Even the media sometimes failed to distinguish between the two. During the 1986 World Series, veteran sportswriter Larry Whiteside, covering the Red Sox for *The Boston Globe,* sidled up to Strawberry and asked for a few words about right-hander Oil Can Boyd.

"Dwight, how do you feel you guys will do against Oil Can?" Whiteside asked innocently.

"He shouldn't be any problem. We'll beat him," said Strawberry, playing right along with Whiteside's mistake. It was a common identification problem—out-of-town reporters interviewing Gooden believing he was Darryl and vice versa.

What was unusual about this episode was that Whiteside is black and admitted, "Of all the people who should've known better, it was me."

For five minutes, Whiteside scribbled furiously into his notebook, recording every word as Strawberry—playfully posing as Gooden—trashed Boyd and the Red Sox. Whiteside walked away, certain, as he put it, "that I had a great story. Everyone said that Dwight was this shy guy, and I'd just gotten him to open up and rip someone in the middle of the World Series."

Whiteside's reportorial instincts finally got the better of him, though. Moments later, he asked someone to point out Gooden and humbly went back for an interview. "Dwight was very polite and made sure he didn't offend anyone," Whiteside said with a smile.

Even members of the New York media could be guilty of confusing the two. Once, on *Kiner's Korner* in 1985, TV broadcaster and Hall of Famer Ralph Kiner repeatedly erred.

"He kept calling me Darryl, but I wasn't about to correct him," Gooden said. "Ralph was too nice of a guy for that. It happened so many times to me and Straw, what was once more?"

Those were better times for both players, as they were for the entire franchise. For seven years, from 1984 to 1990, the Mets were baseball's top organization, winning more games overall than any other team, never finishing lower than second. The Yankees hardly existed in New York's baseball consciousness. All everyone talked about was the Mets. And Doc and Darryl.

The first sign of trouble was the celebration parade after the stunning 1986 World Series victory over the Red Sox. That's when Gooden overslept and missed the entire affair. He still insists drugs weren't the problem, that it was just a hangover. And he was quick to point out, "I made it to the White House a few days later, and a lot of guys on the team didn't show up. No one said anything about that." Still, the alarms were sounded. That winter, Gooden was arrested for brawling with Tampa police. In April 1987, he tested positive for cocaine and was admitted to the Smithers Alcoholism and Treatment Center in New York City. For the next seven years, Gooden remained drug-free, but the foundation of his addiction never changed: he drank more and more, until one day in 1994 the cocaine finally defeated him again.

His downward spiral continued until the mailman delivered a registered letter from Acting Commissioner Bud Selig. Selig's message was brief and brutal: there would be no baseball in 1995; he was suspended. And that, Gooden said, "is when I realized how far I'd fallen."

Strawberry's fall was just as precipitous. Three years after Gooden had checked into Smithers, the right fielder entered the drug center as well. He was there for alcohol abuse, but Strawberry acknowledged he had frequently been using cocaine. The claim of alcoholism, Strawberry admitted years later, "was just a lie" he told the Mets to defuse the drug rumors. Although he wasn't hopelessly addicted at the time, it was a question of semantics. He was using often enough, and Strawberry's romance with the drug accelerated in 1991, the year after he left the Mets and signed with the Dodgers as a free agent. In L.A., his childhood demons were there to greet him.

Former friends, or people who considered themselves friends, attached themselves to Strawberry. Darryl was a magnet, all right: he was flush with cash, having signed a five-year $20 million deal, and was ready to carry the Dodgers on his well-muscled back. It didn't work out that way, not after the first year in L.A. After hitting twenty-eight home runs with ninety-nine RBIs, Strawberry suffered a debilitating back injury and required surgery. Depression came quickly, and his drinking turned into a severe cocaine addiction. "I let myself get out of control when I was playing for the Dodgers," Strawberry said. By 1994—his career having ground to a virtual halt because of recurring back problems—Strawberry entered the Betty Ford Clinic. Only seventy-nine days separated the admission dates of Strawberry and his former teammate Gooden.

There were other factors sabotaging Strawberry's career besides cocaine. His marriage to Lisa Andrews had dissolved after years of angry, sometimes violent domestic disputes. They had wed in 1985, which, ironically, is when the bonds of the friendship between Strawberry and Gooden began to loosen. Darryl and Lisa separated many times, and in 1987 she filed for legal separation and an order of protection. Lisa filed for divorce in 1989, but the two reconciled that year. In 1990, however, during an especially heated dispute, Lisa struck Darryl in the ribs with a fire poker. In response, Strawberry drew a .25 caliber pistol and pointed the gun at his wife's head. Police arrived on the scene, and Strawberry was arrested on suspicion of assault with a deadly weapon. Although no charges were filed, soon after Dr. Allan Lans—the Mets' team psychiatrist—flew to L.A. to counsel Strawberry. Within days, he was admitted to Smithers.

Strawberry says his problems with Lisa were financial. "She was all about money, that's all she ever cared about," he said. The Mets privately believed that had Strawberry's marriage not been so turbulent—indeed, if he'd remained single—he might have been a happier player, perhaps even drug-free.

Then again, maybe not. Strawberry, one of five children, had a history of alcohol abuse on his father's side and said "it was only a matter of time" before his own problems surfaced. Besides, in the eighties at Shea, drinking was part of the Met culture. Hernandez, who had testified at the Pittsburgh drug trials in 1985, admitted he had used cocaine at one time in his career. The caterer in the visiting clubhouse at Three Rivers Stadium had been charged with trafficking cocaine to players of opposing teams, and Hernandez was one of several athletes who admitted to using the drug. Nevertheless, he could be found with a bucketful of ice-cold beers at his locker after every game, washing down every off-the-record comment with another swig of Budweiser.

Like Hernandez, Strawberry took comfort in alcohol. "Every time I've ever gotten in trouble, it's because I was drunk," he said. His worst crisis, however, had nothing to do with drinking or drugs but with the Internal Revenue Service. In January 1994, the U.S. Attorney's Office in White Plains, New York, began investigating members of the 1986 Mets team, acting on a tip that several players had failed to declare income from card-show appearances.

The probe led to Hernandez, David Cone, Dave Magadan, Howard Johnson, Ron Darling, Gooden, and Strawberry. Ultimately, it was Strawberry who was punished, as he pleaded guilty to a felony charge and was sentenced to six months' house arrest, in addition to having to pay back taxes and interest totaling $350,000. The sentence was stunningly gentle—he had walked into the courthouse that day, "pretty much sure that I was going to jail," he recalled—but even so, Darryl's life was in near ruin by April 1995.

At the time of his sentencing, Strawberry was without money, and without an agent, and without a job. The San

Francisco Giants, who had added Strawberry to their roster on July 6, 1994, had released him, following yet another positive drug test in January 1995, just as Strawberry had learned from his attorneys that he was probably going to jail. He stopped speaking to agent Eric Goldschmidt, whom Strawberry claimed had duped him into signing false tax returns. Goldschmidt declined to comment on the charge. Goldschmidt was also facing legal problems with the IRS, although ultimately he would be found not guilty of tax evasion. Strawberry's world was surrounded in crisis, and general managers didn't trust the thirty-three-year-old enough to give him another chance.

No one was sure if he could stay clean. No one knew if he could still hit the fastball. After all, Darryl had totaled just fourteen home runs since 1991, and he was reaching the age where many players lose their skills altogether. Strawberry had a new agent, a New York–based attorney named Bill Goodstein, and, through him, found his last hope as a major leaguer: George Steinbrenner.

For years Strawberry had wondered what it would be like to be a Yankee, to play with Don Mattingly. "I always respected the guy because he was so professional," Strawberry said. "He was a little guy, but tough. Humble, but with a lot of pride. All those years I was with the Mets, I wanted to meet him, be a teammate, get a chance to know why everyone thought he was the greatest."

Well, Strawberry got his chance in June, when the Yankees signed him to a one-year deal for $675,000. In a way, Goodstein had created a miracle, pulling down that much money for Strawberry. Only the White Sox seemed to have much interest in Darryl, and that was partly due to Goodstein's longstanding friendship with team owner Jerry Reinsdorf. Even so, the Sox were only offering the major-league minimum salary of $115,000, so when Steinbrenner essentially bid against himself, Strawberry was his.

Why would The Boss take such a risk? "Because I believe everyone deserves a second chance," Steinbrenner said, although Darryl would later find out Steinbrenner wouldn't always be so benevolent. For now, though, all the Yankees asked was that Strawberry spend a few days playing with their Class A affiliate in Tampa, quicken his swing, and then be ready for a triumphant return to the big leagues.

It would be Darryl's way of showing the Dodgers and Giants they were wrong to release him. It was Steinbrenner's way of showing the baseball world that if no one else could rehabilitate Strawberry, he could. And while he was at it, why not tweak the Mets a little, too? The only problem with Strawberry's assignment to the minor leagues was that he was still under house arrest and, under the terms of his sentencing, was required to remain in his hotel room at all times, including meals. Besides traveling to and from the ballpark, and attending drug and alcohol counseling sessions, Darryl was trapped at the Bay Harbor Inn, Steinbrenner's resort hotel located on the Tampa Bay shore. Strawberry might have been back in baseball, but to the IRS and federal government, he was, in fact, a prisoner.

That's exactly what Gooden learned when he pulled into the parking lot of the Bay Harbor. With him was his friend Vincent Kenyon, a thirty-eight-year-old former stockbroker from New York whose professional career on Wall Street was sabotaged by cocaine and crack in the early nineties. Kenyon had been fighting addiction for nearly three years and had discovered an instant bond with Gooden ever since they were introduced by Doc's new agent, Ray Negron.

It was Kenyon who directed Doc to Narcotics Anonymous in St. Petersburg. It was Kenyon who had helped Gooden understand the depth of his drug addiction—why, after seven years of clean tests with the Mets, he fell again in '94. Kenyon himself had several relapses during the winter and would again go down in the summer of '95, at one point disappearing for three days on a crack binge. And eventually, Gooden and Kenyon would split up over the broker's inability to stay clean. But for now, the two had only one goal that July afternoon: visiting Darryl Strawberry.

Doc, of course, was there to catch up with an old friend; even though they had drifted apart some, the bond was still real. The long hours in a hotel room had to be killing Straw, Gooden thought, so he brought a hot plate and some home-cooked food prepared by his wife, Monica. Kenyon was there to see if he could offer any advice about staying clean, although it had been nearly six months since Strawberry had fallen and there hadn't been any close calls since.

Gooden and Kenyon assumed they would spend an hour or so in Darryl's room and then have dinner with Doc's family in St. Petersburg later that night. That was their first mistake. The two learned as soon as they entered the Bay Harbor Inn that while it might have been a resort hotel to those on vacation or business in the Tampa area, it was a prison to Strawberry.

Gooden reached for the house phone in the lobby and asked for Darryl Strawberry.

"I'm sorry, sir, he's not taking any calls. You can leave a message," the operator told Gooden. He put the phone down and went to the front desk.

"I'm Dwight Gooden, and me and my friend here are supposed to visit Darryl Strawberry," Gooden said patiently. The front desk clerk asked them to repeat their names, copied them on a piece of paper, and then excused herself. When she returned, she was accompanied by a hotel security officer. He was accompanied by a familiar figure from Gooden's past, Arthur Richman.

Richman had been, for several decades, an executive with the Mets. At one time, he was a journalist, the brother of United Press International legend Milton Richman. Arthur eventually became the Mets' public relations chief, then their traveling secretary, and finally one of the club's vice presidents. In 1993, Richman defected to the Yankees' media relations department, and while it wasn't exactly like Leo Durocher trading in his Dodger uniform for the Giants', it was odd seeing Richman become a Steinbrenner employee. Richman, sixty-five, was more of a goodwill ambassador than anything else—at least at the start—and seemed to be on a personal services contract to the Yankee owner.

One of Richman's tasks in 1995 was to oversee Strawberry's return to the big leagues. More accurately, he was there to supervise Darryl's house arrest. Not in any legal way—the Yankees had already hired former Drug Enforcement Agency honcho James Williams to act as a security liaison—but in Strawberry's day-to-day affairs. That meant Richman spent nearly seven weeks on the road with Darryl, living in a hotel room adjoining his.

"I'm too old for this shit," Richman would moan, although he secretly enjoyed the importance the assignment afforded him within the organization. Besides, Darryl was no stranger; he was there when Strawberry broke in with the Mets in 1983, all arms and legs and unharnessed ego. Richman was also on board when Gooden showed up the next spring, which is why Doc expected at least a friendly reception at the Bay Harbor.

Richman was certainly no stranger to crisis control. Everyone in the Mets community remembered that he was asked to rescue one of the club's executives in spring training in 1985, when he was arrested for soliciting a prostitute in Tampa. Through Richman's deft handling of the situation, no charges were ever brought against the official, who is no longer with the team, and the matter died before ever making it to the newspapers.

Richman was a diplomat and a politician and generally considered a good guy. But Gooden found him to be cold and a bit too official when it came to dealing with Strawberry.

"Dwight, how are you?" Richman said indifferently. The two hugged, but there was little friendship in the embrace.

"I'm good, real good, Arthur," Gooden said. "We came to see Darryl."

Richman sighed wearily. "It's not that easy. You can't just walk in and talk to him. We have to clear you first."

Richman went on to explain that Strawberry could not receive visitors unless they were first cleared by his probation officer. And he couldn't even take phone calls directly unless a message was left, usually with Richman, and that person was also cleared. Gooden and Kenyon were forced to wait nearly thirty minutes in the Bay Harbor lobby until phone calls were made—first to the Yankees, then to Darryl's probation officer in California. Finally, Doc and Kenyon were allowed upstairs, but even then the security was oppressive. They found a guard outside Strawberry's room, and the two visitors were forced to show picture ID and sign in. The guard, who sat by Strawberry's door, was on duty twenty-four hours a day.

"Darryl, it's like you're a prisoner of war here," Gooden said with a laugh. Finally, after all these months, the two were standing in the same room. Doc had expected an upbeat, optimistic Strawberry, but instead he found Darryl to be reserved, almost faraway, inside his own skin. Strawberry lived in a two-bedroom suite, sharing the accommodations with Richman. Strawberry's room seemed barely lived in: there were two suitcases, still half packed, a few toilet articles, and the Bible resting on the nightstand next to the bed.

Gooden figured Strawberry would lead a quieter life, especially since he'd come so close to being jailed for his tax problems. That was enough to scare anyone. But even Doc didn't expect Strawberry to have retreated so far from his old personality. There was gospel music coming out of Strawberry's cassette recorder, a far cry from the rap Darryl used to listen to in the Met clubhouse. And when Doc tried again to joke about the lean lifestyle, Strawberry just shook his head.

"This is the way I gotta live now," Darryl said. "I don't care what they make me do, I'm just thankful they're giving me this chance."

"But, Straw, come on, what about that music?" Gooden asked.

"I don't listen to that other stuff anymore," Strawberry said. Doc backed off. Maybe this change was real. Or, if it wasn't, Strawberry had convinced himself it was. This wasn't the first time Strawberry had undergone such a radical metamorphosis. In 1991, he embraced Christianity, a conversion that was met with satisfaction by straight-ahead Mets like Howard Johnson and Tim Teufel. Other Mets weren't so sure, convinced it was just a phase. Gooden was one of the Mets who raised an eyebrow at Darryl's sudden affinity for the heavens, but he never dared criticize Strawberry. That wasn't his way. And now, sitting in Strawberry's hotel room, he politely listened as Darryl tried to teach him about the evils of the world.

"Doc, you gotta listen to me, you have to change. Your whole life has to change," Strawberry said. "If you want to beat this thing, you gotta stay out of the bars, stay away from the ladies who chase ballplayers, you gotta stop drinking. I ain't doing any of those things anymore."

Gooden listened and nodded and told Darryl he understood. It's easy to live that life now, Gooden thought, when there's a cop sitting outside your door. But he didn't dare say that to Strawberry. Gooden knew he was an addict, just like Strawberry, and in no position to pass judgment. It was just that Darryl sounded so sure of himself.

"It's the drinking, Doc. That's what always did it to me," Strawberry said. "I ain't drinking no more. And I'm staying home at night. That's what I learned about all this stuff. Stay away from the stuff that tempted you in the first place. You and me, we aren't strong enough for those temptations. Just stay home. I got one last chance in my career. This is it for me. I'm not going to mess this one up."

Gooden promised Darryl that he, too, was on the way. He was attending Narcotics Anonymous meetings in St. Pete, taking his drug tests three times a week, working out five times a week at Eckerd College. "Darryl, I know what I have to do," Gooden said. But just as Gooden wondered about Strawberry, Darryl had his doubts about his buddy, too. Months later, he said, "I got the feeling Doc was still in denial a little bit about his problem. While I was talking, I got the feeling he was thinking, 'I'm not as bad off as you.'"

All the while, Kenyon sat and listened. After three years of battling cocaine, he knew the difference between commitment and an addict's lies. "I've heard every story under the sun. I've used half of them myself," he said. "But when I listened to Darryl, I truly, truly believed he was free from drugs. I was really impressed with the things he said."

It took about thirty minutes or so, but finally the talk dried up. No one really wanted to bring up the old days—there were too many reminders of the careers that had been wasted. Strawberry said, getting up, "We gotta go forward, Doc." Only no one knew where the long, flat path was leading. The future? Strawberry wasn't even allowed to make plans for dinner. The idea of heading over to Doc's house that night was quashed by the probation people: leaving Tampa for St. Pete would have constituted a violation of his house arrest. So for another night, Darryl would be eating room service, alone in his room.

"I don't mind this, not at all," he told Gooden, hugging him at the door. "After what I've been through, this is easy." Gooden and Kenyon signed out with the guard at Darryl's door and headed back to the parking lot. In a way, Strawberry was right: at least he had baseball in front of him, even with all the trappings of a prison cell. For Gooden, the summer would seem much, much longer. He was out of the game, unemployed, wondering if anyone would believe him when he said he was clean. At least Darryl had George Steinbrenner. Of all people, the Yankee Boss. Would it be so outrageous to think Steinbrenner would want Gooden, too? Doc shook his head, starting the monstrous engine of his BMW. The Yankees? Impossible, he thought.

3

IN THE
BEGINNING (DARRYL)

THE MEDICAL NAME was Dexedrine, but they were better known as white crosses, little white tablets that could fill a ballplayer with hope and illusion. They could defeat any hangover, any sleepless night, numb the effects of any domestic quarrel. The crosses were a major leaguer's champions, known to doctors as amphetamines but referred to more affectionately in the clubhouses: if you didn't call them white crosses, then they were beanies or, even more commonly, beans.

You took beans with coffee. That way, the amphetamine rush was turbocharged by caffeine. Magically, about thirty minutes before game time, even after the sorriest of batting-practice sessions, bat speed was restored, legs moved faster, the heart went off on a race. Of course, it was possible to play baseball without beans: you just had to get enough sleep and at least moderate the late-night drinking. But it was easier not to. As Darryl Strawberry came to realize in the late 1980s, the beans were too powerful to live without.

Strawberry started in 1984, when, one day, feeling unusually sluggish, he decided: why not? There was already a quiet fraternity of Mets who used amphetamines, not junkies by any means but players who didn't mind taking a shortcut. Actually, it was more like having it both ways at Shea: booze and baseball coexisting magnificently with the great equalizer, beans. And as long as the Mets kept dominating . . . well, who really minded? Strawberry estimated, "About half the guys were doing it, and some of them started to believe they couldn't play unless they were high on 'em." At least two Mets became so addicted they didn't even wait until batting practice to start ingesting the pills. They would start using around noon and show up at the park for a night game already at full-blast.

Amphetamine use in baseball goes back decades, back to at least the fifties, when the drug was called "greenies." Jim Bouton described in great detail in *Ball Four* how the Yankees, including Mickey Mantle, relied on greenies. So did Pete Rose. It seemed everyone did. The expression was: "Go to the jar." And in the eighties, especially the early eighties, baseball was experiencing the same mass experimentation with cocaine as the rest of the country. So what difference did it make if Darryl Strawberry was using amphetamines, too? In Straw's case, however, amphetamines were a stepping-stone to a much larger problem, specifically cocaine. And rarely had drugs undercut a player with so much talent. As teammate Ed Lynch said, "The first time I saw Darryl in the batting cage, the very first time, I said to myself, My God, that guy's going to Cooperstown."

Strawberry often wondered where his career might have gone had it not been for drugs and alcohol, so many at-bats, so many games, so many weeks and months lost to lethargy, lack of focus, or just pure exhaustion. "There were long, long stretches that I couldn't keep my focus; concentrating was impossible," he said. "Sometimes baseball was the last thing on my mind." Darryl had the gift of making baseball look easy—his running stride, his swing, even the way he threw the ball from the outfield had an inner-city hipness to it. There was never any rage to him; Met fans never saw Strawberry throw a bat or a helmet or argue too vehemently with an umpire. Fans thought he was lazy or indifferent, especially in contrast to players like Gregg Jefferies, who regarded each at-bat as a personal apocalypse. What is true is that Strawberry often gave away his first and second at-bats in a game, looking bad even on middle-of-the-plate strikes. That's why so many pitchers made the mistake of trying to defeat Strawberry the same way all four at-bats in a game. Somehow, he would become a different hitter in his third and fourth time up, solving the very same pitches that had made him so helpless early in the game. He had extraordinary power to the opposite field. When Strawberry exercised the discipline to go the other way, he was as explosive as any home-run hitter in the game in the eighties.

Still, there was something about Strawberry's on-field demeanor that made it impossible for so many to embrace him. Maybe it was the contrast to franchise crowd pleaser and perpetual nice guy Mookie Wilson or to the purity that Gary Carter projected. Those two, along with Dave Magadan and Tim Teufel, were the forces of light among the Mets. No one ever had to produce a list of Mets who were drinking too much or using beans. You just knew the ones who were definitely clean. They rode at the front of the bus and the plane, where players actually tried to sleep. They returned to the hotel on the road before dawn, their postgame activity restricted to a bite to eat at an all-night diner. Carter, Teufel, and Wilson were part of the Mets' Bible squad, although Magadan, raised as a Catholic, was more of a secularist than anything else.

No one disliked Mookie. No one could. He was happy, seemingly sin-free, never drawn into the tabloids' clubhouse game of He Said, What Do You Say? in which reporters would subtly provoke players into an overheated quote. Even the most cynical of inner-circle Mets found he was beyond reproach, although Ron Darling said, "The thing about Mookie was that, at times, he would be in another universe. You'd pitch a great game, and he wouldn't even acknowledge you in the dugout." But the other Mets . . . well, they were targets. Carter was too clean, too image-conscious. Teufel was too passive, too. And Magadan drew the kiss of death from Strawberry in 1987 when he said the first baseman wasn't competitive enough, or as he put it, Magadan had "too much sugar in his blood."

What Magadan—and Carter and Wilson and Teufel—did not have in their blood, most certainly, was amphetamines. "I believe now, looking back, it was widespread, but the funny thing is, I never saw it going on in the clubhouse," Magadan said. "I mean, it's not like guys were lining up at the water fountain with pills in their hands, waiting to get high. No one wanted to be open about it. It was, obviously, a very secretive thing."

The beans came from outside the clubhouse, that much was certain. The Mets' physicians and trainers were, by law, prohibited from dispensing the drugs, but they had some tacit knowledge that players were doing more than drinking coffee to cope with the endless blur of games and road trips. "To be honest, I'm not sure where the amphetamines came from," said former trainer Steve Garland. "They're a controlled substance, and New York is one of the tougher states to be trafficking in controlled substances. As a part of the Mets' staff, obviously this is one thing the players didn't want me to know about."

Strawberry was easy prey for the beans, especially since he had started experimenting with cocaine as early as his rookie year in 1983. He'd arrived in New York as a franchise savior with a reputation of being a street-smart homeboy from South-Central L.A. But anyone who met Darryl knew, instantly, he was no tough guy, just a softhearted kid open to suggestion. "Darryl was someone who always wanted to be liked," said his mother, Ruby. Indeed, if any pattern marked Strawberry's upbringing, it was his vulnerability to outside influences. Darryl rarely got angry, rarely said no. He loved kids. He was nice to fans. He was nice to almost everyone. Although Strawberry flirted with cocaine in 1983—introduced to him, he says, by two veterans who said, "It was the thing to do in the big leagues"—his drug of choice through the eighties was amphetamines. It seemed so many other Mets were doing them; everyone else was living a hard nightlife, too. Darryl just pushed it a little further.

"Until that point, I had no idea about taking amphetamines," he said. "I mean, I drank beer in high school, drank beer in the minor leagues, just like everyone else. I wasn't a saint, but I wasn't a junkie. But no one ever told me amphetamines were what you did in the big leagues to get by. I didn't know one way or another about them. So I tried 'em. It helped me get by when I was feeling bad or hung over. Little by little, I started using more of them because everyone else was. It was sort of the thing to do with our team."

Even manager Davey Johnson kept a supply of vodka in his office refrigerator. Johnson drank with his coaches—both at home and on the road. Drinking was countenanced from top to bottom, and even the tradition that mandated players stay away from the hotel bar was waived under Davey's administration. Most managers preferred having the hotel bar to themselves, where they could drink in peace and not have to listen to a drunk player complain about his contract or a lack of innings or demand a trade. But Davey always said, "I want my guys close to home, so if anyone gets into trouble, I can at least make sure things don't get out of hand."

It wasn't a common occurrence, but the Mets could, from time to time, see Johnson work his way through a night of alcohol. Strawberry only half kiddingly said, "Davey was as wild as the rest of us. Shoot, he was lit, too." Ten years later, Johnson admitted, "I did my share of drinking when I was with the Mets. Probably too much drinking. But it was my way of dealing with the pressure. I don't know of a manager who's come and gone through New York who hasn't, at some time, had to drink to cope. I learned: I stopped drinking. But not until after I left."

Johnson, with firsthand knowledge of what pressure meant in New York and what it could drive a player to do, kept his rules simple in the clubhouse: show up on time and win. There were no curfews, no punishment for showing up hungover, no coaching-staff spies working the hotel lobby checking to see who the last player in was. If you performed, you had free rein over the other side of midnight. Johnson was proud of his philosophy, which stated, "I treat my players like men." Besides, Davey already knew who was doing what, just by how much a player suffered in batting practice the next day. The ones who cared showed up early for extra batting practice, if for no other reason than to sweat out the toxins. As Teufel put it, "There were a lot of guys who were out there at two and three o'clock, feeling like garbage. But they were there because they knew if they'd been out, somewhere you had to pay the price. What bothered us about Darryl is that he brought the effects of his drinking into the game the next day."

Here is where Johnson and Strawberry would wage their war throughout the eighties: over Darryl's inability, or at least his unwillingness, to play the day after a binge. There was no mistaking Darryl's bad days. In fact, they started soon after a game, when Strawberry would have "five or six beers right there, before I headed out the door." Darryl wasn't alone. Hernandez had his beers-in-a-bucket, and everyone else pounded the complimentary Budweiser in the players' lounge. If that wasn't enough, on the way out the door beers were packed in sanitary socks, the cotton stretched obscenely by the weight of thirty-six more ounces. "Go-beers," they were called.

"By the end of the night, I'd have had nine or ten beers like it was nothing," Strawberry said. "I liked getting drunk. It made me feel good. I was happy. I was a happy drunk. But I was sneaky about it. No one knew how drunk I was getting or how often."

Strawberry might have thought he was concealing his alcohol problem, but there was no mistaking his hangover the next day, when he would be the last player in the clubhouse and the first in the trainer's room. Bundled up, sprawled out on the trainer's table, Strawberry would pass the word to Johnson that he wasn't feeling well enough to play. Darryl's Achilles' heel came on Sunday afternoons, when it was almost a given—trainer Garland would be dispatched into Johnson's office with word from the right fielder that he was ill.

Johnson had loved Darryl in his early years and, in many ways, continued to show affection until Strawberry left New York as a free agent in 1990. But nothing infuriated the manager more than a white flag from Strawberry. Johnson would tell Garland, "Fuck him, he's playing. Tell Darryl he's playing," later explaining, "I wanted Straw to know he wasn't the one who was making out the lineup card. I didn't care how hung over he was. It was my decision, not his."

Davey was in the worst sort of predicament with Strawberry. He was the manager and needed to flex some clubhouse muscle with Darryl; in 1992 Jeff Torborg would learn the hard way what an out-of-control team—even if the core of malcontents numbered no more than two, Eddie Murray and Vince Coleman—could do to the perception of a manager's authority. But Johnson also knew Strawberry was troubled by a fatherless upbringing and, more than anything, needed guidance from an older, stable male figure. It was no coincidence that Strawberry's first attachment as a Met in 1983 was to then hitting coach Jimmy Frey, a short, balding man from another generation and another social pedigree but one who sure knew his hitting and was more than patient with Strawberry.

They looked like an odd pair, Strawberry and Frey, a biracial Mutt and Jeff. But Strawberry was just an impressionable rookie in 1983, and as Frey was to say years later, "I really felt like Darryl was all alone and needed a friend." A lonely superstar? For all the power in his swing, for all the graceful lines in his 6-6, 215-pound body, Strawberry was, even in his thirties, still the same kid who had trouble talking to girls in high school and who took fifteen years to get over the fact that his father had left home when Darryl was twelve.

Darryl had always needed to be part of a group, which is why if the group drank beer, as it did in the minor leagues, so did he. The amphetamines were next, in the mid-eighties, as he was progressing from beer to hard liquor. By the late

1980s, Darryl had advanced to cocaine. Only in 1990 did he realize, "I was on a pace to kill myself."

STRAWBERRY WAS THE middle child in a family of five: he had two older brothers, Michael and Ron, and two younger sisters, Regina and Michelle. "We were a close, relatively normal family," Darryl's mother, Ruby, said. She was, and remains, an energetic and charismatic woman who worked for the phone company and was forced to raise her family on her own when Henry Strawberry, a postal worker, left the house after they were divorced in 1974.

The Strawberrys lived in a small house near Seventh Avenue in Compton, less than two miles from Dodger Stadium. Darryl was obviously an athlete, showing signs even as early as eleven or twelve that sports were his passion. He played baseball and basketball, just like his brothers, who were just as devoted to sports. All three modeled themselves after their father, who was a gifted athlete himself. Henry Strawberry would bring the boys to his softball games in a league in Manchester Park, and it wasn't long before Darryl developed a bond with baseball.

"His whole life, as far back as I can remember, Darryl's goal was to be involved with baseball," said Ruby Strawberry. "Baseball meant more to Darryl than school or girls or anything else. He was so shy otherwise, but baseball seemed to make him happy." Even in his teens, Strawberry had that long, looping swing that would later make him such a home-run threat in the big leagues. One of Darryl's best boyhood friends and a teammate at Crenshaw High School, Eric Davis, would also make it to the big leagues someday, and the two became teammates in L.A. in 1993. But Davis never had the gift of Strawberry's swing. Even then he admired it.

"You could look at a film of Darryl hitting the ball in high school and one of him today, and it wouldn't be much different," Davis said. "There's not too many players who've gone through their whole careers with one swing. But Darryl has. His swing was a natural."

But there were hurdles on the way to the 1980 draft, when the Mets made Strawberry their number-one pick. The turbulence in Strawberry's life began with his father's departure from the house. Darryl's oldest brother, Ronnie, said, "We looked up to our father, he was our inspiration. That was our problem." When the elder Strawberry left, Ronnie said, "There went our happiness." Ruby remembered how sweetly the relationship had started thirty-five years ago, even in the way she and Henry met. "I asked him what his name was, and when he told me it was Henry Strawberry, I laughed out loud. I thought it was a joke," she said. "I mean, who could possibly have a name like Strawberry? My maiden name was Jones, so it was a little difficult for me to believe Darryl's father at first."

Ruby insisted, "There wasn't a lot of fighting that went on between me and Henry, at least not until the end, when we got separated." But Darryl said, in a different recollection, "I felt like I'd been through some abuse when I was a kid. Mostly, my father yelled a lot. He drank a lot. At the end, he wasn't paying much attention to me or my brothers and sisters. Looking back, I can see now that addiction ran in my family. My father definitely had an alcohol problem, and it's something I've had to deal with because of him."

But Strawberry's mother believed that, apart from alcohol, her husband's gambling had become a cancer to the marriage, although Henry would later say he never made enough money to bet it away. Either way, Darryl was at his most vulnerable age when his father left: twelve going on thirteen and desper-

ate for someone to depend on. Ronnie, although still interested in sports, was already involved with gangs. Not long
after Henry Strawberry left, Darryl began taking an interest in
that lifestyle.

Ronnie Strawberry pleaded with his brother to stay away,
but the impressionable Darryl was slowly being drawn in. Finally, Ronnie actually began beating his brother as a way to
keep him safe. "I would jump him, punch him out, anything
to get Darryl to go home," Ronnie told the *Los Angeles Times*
in 1990. "The people I hung out with, they were athletically
gifted, but mentally, they shut it down. I didn't want Darryl
to ever shut it down."

Yet there didn't seem to be a way for Strawberry to get
over the hurt of losing his father. It was as if he took his parents' divorce personally. "It hurt me real bad that my father
would leave us like that," Darryl said. "It's something that
took me a long time to get over and come to terms with.
Why? Why? I asked myself all the time why I didn't have a
father anymore, how he could do that to us. No one
should go through what I went through, growing up without a father."

"Darryl did take it hard," his mother conceded. "He had a
lot of hostility that I didn't know about. All I knew then was,
I would be at my office, and the kids would call me, screaming about the fights going on in the house, I would be telling
them there was nothing I could do about it. Looking back,
there were so many things I should've been aware of, his need
for attention. Every fall I used to take my kids for clothes for
school—nice stuff, the best I could afford. But every day Darryl was sent home from school because he wore cutoff jeans
and sweatpants. He wouldn't wear the clothes that I had
bought for him. I would ask him, 'Darryl, why aren't you

wearing the new clothes?' and he would say, 'Mom, I don't know why.' " To this day, Strawberry cannot explain rejecting the clothes, only saying, "It didn't feel right wearing them."

It was baseball that eventually rescued Strawberry, although even his love of the game was no match for his mood swings. Darryl had already made a name for himself in Compton's Little Leagues and junior leagues, thanks to one of his first mentors, John Mosely. Interestingly, Mosely, who was fifty-eight at the time and a city-employed truck driver, believed Darryl was "probably the worst" athlete in the family. But one day, at Athens Park on El Segundo Avenue, Mosely said, "Darryl hit a soccer player about five hundred feet away with a fly ball. I said to him, 'Boy, you've got everything but a good head.' "

Eventually, Crenshaw High School coach Brooks Hurst had his first meeting with Darryl, although it was only through Michael Strawberry that their lives intersected. Hurst had pulled up to the Strawberrys' house to pick up Michael to attend a Dodgers game when he saw the tall, lonely Darryl, the one with all the physical gifts but a bad attitude. "I'd never seen Darryl before," Hurst told the *L.A. Times.* "I shouted at him if he wanted to join us. He said yes, and he jumped in the van.

"I'll never forget how that whole game, while the other boys were running around the stadium, Darryl just sat there and stared at the field." A year later, as a 6-4 sophomore—taller than anyone in his family—Strawberry was playing for Hurst at Crenshaw and his shyness had only worsened. There was something rebellious about Strawberry that both intrigued and angered Hurst, just as it would do to Davey Johnson a decade later. Hurst certainly didn't dislike Darryl, but he realized there was a problem, even in his very first season.

"You could tell Darryl was going to be a great player, but there was so much friction between us," Hurst said. "He would go halfhearted through his drills. He was supposed to be swinging at a tire, but he would be staring at another field or up in the sky." Hurst lost his patience with Strawberry that same year because, between innings, it took the sixteen-year-old outfielder "a full one and a half minutes" to return to the dugout from the outfield.

Feeling as though he needed to make an example of Strawberry, Hurst confronted him, pointed to the C on his cap, and shouted, "Don't you see that C? Don't you know what it stands for? It means you've got to hustle." In a reaction that would be repeated many times in his future, Strawberry simply removed his jersey, tossed it on the bench, and said, "I quit." He didn't return to the Crenshaw team until his junior year.

Hurst later recalled that almost immediately after the game, Strawberry had recovered from his tantrum and wanted to return to the team. But the coach refused. "It would have blown my credibility with the team and ultimately hurt Darryl," he remembered. "Even the principal came to me to find out how come I wouldn't let him play, but I just told the principal, 'It's something I have to do. I have no choice.'"

Only once he returned as a junior did Strawberry begin to have a future in baseball. He hit .372 with five home runs and was 4-1 as a pitcher, and scouts began following him everywhere. All the while, Ruby Strawberry spent long days with the phone company, unaware of the commotion her son was creating. She recalled, "One day, I picked up the paper, and there it was, a story about Darryl being the best high school player in the country. I said, 'Darryl, is this true?' I had no idea," she said. "He was just too shy to talk about how good he'd become."

But the rest of the country was paying attention to the long-limbed prospect from L.A. who was so self-doubting and shy he sidled up to Hurst one day at practice and asked innocently, "So you really think I'm worth all this?" The Mets apparently thought so. As baseball's lowliest franchise in 1979, they earned the right to the number-one pick in the June amateur draft and had no doubt Strawberry was their target. The Mets were just shadows of the Yankees at that time, eclipsed by Billy Martin, Reggie Jackson, Goose Gossage, and, of course, George Steinbrenner. Met ownership detested Steinbrenner's obsession with keeping his Yankees on the back page and certainly his recklessness in the free-agent market. But even Nelson Doubleday, Jr., and Fred Wilpon had to admit the Mets were no match for the Yankees, who were on their way to another Eastern Division crown in 1980.

Maybe that's one reason Strawberry stood out so early as a Met: he was the franchise's answer to Reggie, to Steinbrenner—to everything the Mets had not been for seven years, since their last World Series, in 1973. No one knew for sure how long Strawberry would remain in the minor leagues, but the Met front office understood the sooner Darryl arrived in New York, the sooner they could promote him to their success-starved public. The possibilities were endless: with a name like Strawberry and a public relations guru in Jay Horwitz, it wouldn't be long before the Yankees were back-page history in the city. At least that was the plan.

But Strawberry suffered from severe homesickness in his first summer away from Los Angeles. "I hated it. I was lost," he said simply. "Darryl was calling home every single day, telling me he was ready to quit and come home," said Ruby Strawberry. "I knew there was something wrong because he'd never called me so many times like that in his life." In 1981,

Crenshaw coach Hurst received a call from Mets general manager Frank Cashen, who said Strawberry had disappeared from his Class A team and no one could find him. Cashen asked Hurst for help, for any clue in locating the wayward prospect.

Hurst had no idea where Strawberry was, but he wasn't entirely surprised—certainly not when Strawberry returned to the team in Kingsport, Tennessee, explaining that he'd been considering quitting baseball and turning to basketball. His Class A manager, Gene Dusan, said, "Darryl never actually left the team, but he wasn't putting all his marbles in the jar. He wasn't hustling like he should, he wasn't pushing like he should, and I let him know it."

The next day, Strawberry walked into Dusan's office and said, "You going to be at the office at three tomorrow?" Dusan recalled. "He rarely got to the ballpark that early, so I knew he was changed. From then on, I have never dealt with a better player."

There was money in Darryl's future. No one disputed his earning potential, certainly not after his 1982 season at Double-A in Jackson, Mississippi, where he hit .283 with thirty-four home runs and ninety-seven RBIs. Of course, Strawberry struck out an astounding 145 times in 435 at-bats, but he was clearly the club's most potent home-run prospect. And there was no hint of trouble in Strawberry's personal life either, especially since he was being represented by one of baseball's most respected agents of the 1980s, Richman Bry. Based in St. Louis, Bry had first learned of Strawberry when he was a senior at Crenshaw and an article on him appeared in *Sports Illustrated*.

It was an easy phone call for Bry to make after reading the article about the country's top high school prospect: there was Ruby Strawberry's name, the phone company she worked for in Los Angeles, Strawberry's high school, and his coach.

"I figured it was a one-in-a-million chance, but why the hell not at least try?" Bry said. "Within five minutes, I had Ruby on the phone, and after talking to her, I got the impression no one else had even tried to reach her. I was astounded. So I asked her, 'Would you and Darryl like to go to a game at Dodger Stadium?' She said yes. Of course, I pulled out all the stops."

That included a visit from San Diego Chargers star Kellen Winslow, one of Bry's highest-profile clients. St. Louis shortstop Garry Templeton, another star in Bry's stable, also stopped by to say hello to Strawberry (the Dodgers were hosting the Cardinals that night). After the game, Strawberry was introduced to former Cardinals star and Hall of Famer Lou Brock, yet another Bry showpiece, in the broadcast booth. Afterward, Strawberry dined with Bry, Brock, Winslow, and Templeton, and, as a finishing touch, Bry handed the keys to his car to his son Rich junior and told him and Darryl to enjoy a night out on the town.

"The next day, my son, who was a freshman at USC at the time, called me and said, 'Dad, we got him,' " Bry said. "I said, 'Richie, I haven't made a follow-up phone call yet.' He said, 'Don't worry. You definitely got him.' " Strawberry was won over by the younger Bry's sincerity and the fact that he didn't push too hard on his father's behalf. They had a few beers, they talked women and sports. Strawberry, who trusted easily, had seen and heard enough to give the elder Bry his business. That evening, Bry and Ruby Strawberry had a handshake agreement, and the two soon negotiated a $200,000 deal from the Mets. Over the years, Strawberry and Bry enjoyed a close friendship, until 1988, when Strawberry left his agent for the combative Eric Goldschmidt. It's not an unusual turn of events in baseball, players bouncing from agent to agent, the new guy always promising more than the last and the player always believing the seduction line. Bry knew, sooner or later, he would lose Darryl. He said, "Somehow, I still think we're friends. But I did notice over the course of time, Darryl was starting to drink too much. Nothing outrageous, but five-six-seven drinks every time we went out to dinner. He never seemed drunk, though. That's what seemed so odd. He was drinking and never showing any effects. I know athletes can be like that. But a couple of times, I said, 'Darryl, maybe you should get some help.' Darryl would just laugh it off. He said. 'Nah, I'm fine. There's nothing wrong.' He would just sweet-talk me. Darryl was always good at that."

4

IN THE
BEGINNING (DWIGHT)

HE WAS A senior at Hillsborough High School in
Tampa, just seventeen, and already reaching the mid-
eighties with his fastball. Friends remember Dwight
Gooden as shy, but on the mound he had just the right
amount of arrogance. A good heater will do that to a
pitcher, make him feel invincible. Heavyweights with
the big knockout punch have that same fuck-you swag-
ger. Gooden said, "Ever since I was thirteen or fourteen,
when I started to realize I could strike hitters out whenever I wanted to, nothing ever matched that feeling."

But off the field, Doc was a different person, not particularly slick with girls, a little too eager to be liked,
raised in gentler surroundings than Strawberry. If anything, Gooden was sheltered by his generous parents.
Still, like most teens, Doc was curious about the world
around him, and he was particularly intrigued about the
phenomenon that was growing at Hillsborough High

School, his neighborhood in Tampa, and all around the country in 1982: cocaine.

The source of Gooden's curiosity was a dealer who hung around the high school. Everyone knew him: he was in his mid-thirties, an alumnus of the school, smart, slick, and he drove an unmistakable black Mercedes. Gooden had, through his junior year, resisted drugs, even marijuana, but a number of friends had tried cocaine and liked it. Doc was teetering. "I kept hearing from them, 'Come on, man, just once. You can't really be scared of the shit, are you?' " Gooden said.

Doc had reached a crossroads in his upbringing, when drinking beer while riding around with friends was no longer enough to satisfy the group's hip quotient. Cocaine had become a fad, and Gooden had to decide how long he could go before succumbing to peer pressure. He never thought of consulting his parents; that was out of the question. His high school coach, Billy Reed? How could Doc explain he was curious about drugs? Gooden certainly knew how his friends felt. So one day he finally listened to the darker angels of his soul.

It was after practice, around 5 P.M., when Gooden found the dealer, who called himself Hawk, for reasons no one knew. Hawk's eyes widened in surprise when he saw Doc approach.

"Dwight Gooden, everything cool with you?" he asked. "You throwing the shit out of the ball this year, you know that, my man?"

"Thanks, man. I appreciate that," Gooden said, a forced smile frozen on his lips. He was nervous and stuttering badly. "Look, man, I think I wanna buy. You got some of that shit?"

"You? You wanna buy?"

"Yeah," Gooden said, horrified by his own collapse. "What do you got?"

Another dealer would have been all too glad to help Gooden go down. But Hawk was a different drug trafficker. He knew Gooden, followed his athletic career, and had boasted to other dealers that he did *not* sell drugs to Tampa's best ballplayer. But now Gooden was standing before him, ready to be corrupted. In truth, all Doc wanted was to experience the moment, not necessarily the cocaine. He would say years later, "I wanted to get as close to using without ever actually doing the stuff. My intention that day was to buy, and that would be it. I wasn't going any further."

At least Gooden could tell his friends he'd been to see Hawk, copped, and maybe then fake his way around the question when someone asked how he liked cocaine. But the meeting with Hawk turned out differently than Gooden ever planned.

"Well, little brother, I'll hook you up, but we ain't doing nothing right here. Let's you and me take a little walk," Hawk said. They walked several blocks to the black Mercedes. Hawk motioned for Gooden to get in. The car had dark-tinted windows, oversized wheels, and chrome rims. Gooden knew the car was an obvious drug vehicle. Any cop could see that. Gooden wondered how he had allowed himself to lose control of the situation.

"What's the matter, you nervous?" Hawk asked. He was smiling at Gooden. In fact, he was almost sneering at the teenager. Gooden couldn't let Hawk know of his fear—that would be the worst fate of all. So he merely shook his head and said, "Nah, I'm fine." And that closed off Doc's last avenue of escape.

The two men drove for several minutes, although neither one spoke until they pulled up to an apartment building deep in the Belmont Heights neighborhood. Gooden looked at Hawk, waiting for instructions.

"You see that apartment, the one on the third floor, on the corner?" Hawk said, pointing to the building.

"Yeah, I see it," Gooden said, still unsure of the trafficker's intention. He was scared now and didn't care if Hawk knew it. But Doc was several long blocks from home and only wanted the moment to end as quickly as possible. Running out of the car would only deepen his predicament. Better to go along, Gooden decided, and be smarter next time.

"What you're gonna do is go up to three-C, and a couple of my guys will take care of you," Hawk said. "They're waiting for you."

"Waiting for me? They know I'm coming?" Gooden asked.

"Just do what I tell you," Hawk said. "Go."

Gooden wanted to say no, to tell Hawk he'd made a terrible mistake, run home to his parents. But what if the dealer ever told his friends? What would Gooden say then? At seventeen, reputation is everything, a fact that Hawk did not let go unnoticed. In fact, Hawk liked Gooden and was fully aware that he was baptizing a naïve, inexperienced buyer. Hawk knew Doc's senses were being overloaded at that very moment—every sight and sound and thought would remain with him forever. So he decided to make this a lesson Gooden would never forget.

Hawk had, indeed, sold drugs to Hillsborough High School students, plenty of them. But never to a star athlete. And he really didn't want to start now, being that he was a sports fan. The moment Gooden left the car, he walked to a pay phone and called his compatriots in the apartment.

"In about thirty seconds, Dwight Gooden is gonna knock on the door," Hawk said.

"Gooden? The high school kid?" a voice on the other end of the phone asked.

"Yeah, him. He thinks he wants to buy," Hawk said.

"Get the fuck outta here."

"Fuck that, I ain't selling him shit," Hawk said. "But I want you to fuck him up a little. Don't hurt him. But teach the motherfucker a lesson."

Moments later, Gooden knocked at the door. "Hawk sent me," he called, trying to sound fearless and failing miserably.

The door opened, and three well-muscled men, all in their thirties, stood in front of Gooden, staring hard at him. Doc broke off eye contact immediately, but before he did, he noticed the apartment was barely furnished: just a few chairs, a table, and a telephone. There was an awkward silence before Gooden finally said, "Hawk said you got something for me."

"Oh, yeah, we do," said the first man, smiling now. There was something odd about the smile. That was the last thing Gooden remembered. The next instant, he felt a blow to his face so devastating that his eyes rolled back in his head. He lost his footing and for a half second could have sworn he was flying. An instant later, he crashed onto the hardwood floor, the wind knocked out of him.

Gooden was desperate for air, his lungs momentarily incapable of functioning. Even in his panic, Gooden could still feel the warm trail of blood trickling into his mouth. He only wondered if the punch had broken his nose. Gooden had been in minor scuffles in high school, but no one had ever hit him this hard, and he was embarrassed he went down so easily.

He stayed down, too. There was no point in fighting three men, especially if one of them could punch like that. Gooden hoped the dealers would take mercy on him now, so he waited, trying to breathe, not daring to look up. But he immediately realized he had no choice because a hand grabbed the back of his shirt and pulled his face upward toward the ceiling.

Gooden was suddenly staring into Hawk's face, and this time it was tight with anger.

"Listen, motherfucker, the next time you wanna come around here and buy my shit, I might just sell it to you," he said, inches from Gooden's terrified eyes. "Now get the fuck out of here."

DWIGHT EUGENE GOODEN learned about baseball like most kids, from his father. At the age of six, Dan Gooden started taking Dwight to the park in Hillsborough, where they would engage in the time-honored tradition of playing catch. Dan Gooden had the long, easy motion of a pitcher, which he had been as a sandlot player in Americus, Georgia, twenty years earlier. His son had a naturally strong arm, but he loved to hit, and every afternoon at the park would end up with Dwight with a bat in his hand, learning how to hit line drives as his father tossed gentle, middle-of-the plate fastballs to him.

Dan Gooden had a long-range plan for his son. Even when Dwight was four and the family was watching the Atlanta Braves on TV, Dan would say, "Dwight, someday you'll be out there with the pros." His wife, Ella, would roll her eyes because she'd heard it so many times before.

"What about school, getting an education?" Ella Gooden would say. "There's more to this life than baseball."

Not to Dan Gooden. Not only had he been a semipro player, but before that, so had been Dwight's grandfather. Dan Gooden never went further than the sandlots, though, and soon married Ella Mae Jones, a nurse. Dan found a job at a chemical plant outside Tampa. The couple had a quiet, untroubled marriage, raising five children. Unlike Strawberry, Dwight Gooden never experienced any domestic difficulties.

His parents didn't fight, and throughout his entire upbringing, they remained together, as they are today. Dwight was the youngest in the family, and from the beginning, he was treated as such, even to the point of being pampered.

The first real money-earning job Gooden ever had was with the Mets. Until then, his life had been filled only with baseball. "Actually, when I was in high school, my mom brought home job applications for me to fill out, but my dad never let me touch them," Gooden said. "To him, it was more important that I play baseball. Working would've just gotten in the way of the plan. Even with little chores around the house, like cutting the grass, my dad would tell me, 'Just go onto the field, and I'll say you did it.' I never had to make my bed, wash the car, fold my clothes. None of it."

If it hadn't been for cutting avocados off trees—and then selling them by the basket in the parking lot of the local grocery store—Gooden would never have earned a dime before being drafted by the Mets. When the avocados ran out, Gooden and his friends would hang around the grocery store, wait for shoppers on their way out, and offer to carry the groceries to their cars. At the end of the day, Gooden would stuff a few dollars in his pocket and head home, where a hot meal and Mom and Dad awaited.

Gooden lived in the Belmont Heights section of Tampa, a lower-income neighborhood comprised of closely bunched, ranch-style homes. Although the neighborhood's playgrounds today serve as meeting grounds for drug dealers, twenty years ago Belmont Heights was a safe place to live.

"All the families seemed to know each other," said Floyd Youmans, one of Gooden's childhood friends who went on to the major leagues himself. "If you did something wrong, even if you kept a secret from your own mother, someone else's momma would find out. If you concentrated on sports and things like that, it was a good place to grow up, with a lot of good kids around."

In this friendly environment, there was nothing in Gooden's way to block the path to a baseball career. And like Strawberry's, Doc's friends were on a similar track. Among Gooden's circle was Youmans, who threw a ninety-five-mile-per-hour fastball in a five-year career with the Expos and Phillies in the mid- to late eighties. Gooden was also friends with Vance Lovelace, whose career as a reliever would take him to the California Angels and Seattle Mariners between 1988 and 1990. And there was Albert Everett, whose brother Carl would eventually play for the New York Mets in 1995.

By the time Gooden was twelve, he was already overpowering his peers. "It was a joke how much better he was than everyone at that age," Youmans said. "It was like he was already in high school and the hitters were five-year-olds. It was obvious he was on his way to a professional career, but the funny thing is, Dwight never talked about being a major leaguer. None of us did. We actually had too much fun playing in Little League and in high school to think about the future."

Gooden was a third baseman in those days, his powerful arm matched by an equally potent bat. It didn't hurt his budding career that his father was now his coach, too. At the Little League level, Gooden was one of Tampa's best players, but in high school, like Strawberry, Doc had problems with the varsity team. He ran into Billy Reed, Hillsborough's tough disciplinarian coach, who found Gooden to be spoiled and pampered. "He had a problem with Dwight. In fact he had a problem with all of us," Youmans said. "Hillsborough had never really had any real good black ballplayers before, and I guess Billy wanted to prove he wasn't going to play favorites with us."

In his sophomore year, Reed made Gooden pitch batting practice but never allowed him to hit. In the intrasquad games, Gooden was forced to play the field for both teams and again never got to bat. "For some reason, he was punishing me. Maybe because I was one of the youngest guys, I don't know," Gooden said. He was sure of this much: at age fifteen and still eligible for the senior bracket of Tampa's Little League—where Dan Gooden was still a coach—Doc wasn't in the mood to be embarrassed. Without hesitating, he quit the Hillsborough team and returned to the Little League, where he was once again the dominant player.

Reed sneered at Gooden, telling another coach at Hillsborough, "Gooden just wants to play with the little guys. That's where he belongs. Let him go." Dan Gooden accepted his son back, but at school a cold war set in. Reed sent word to Doc that there would be no point in ever returning to the team. "No one quits on me," Reed said. Doc's high school career might have ended there, but his pride forced him to act. Doc prepared to move into his sister Betty's house across town, making him eligible to attend rival Robertson High School. There, another black coach ran a strong program, equal to Reed's. His name was Dave Best, and Gooden let mutual friends know he would pitch for Best and make it a point to beat Reed and Hillsborough.

Reed considered that possibility, then relented, asking Gooden to return to Hillsborough. But their war wasn't finished. Reed made Gooden play in the school's winter league, made him work out during the Christmas holidays and practice with the freshmen and sophomores and players switching to new positions. Youmans said, "It was probably the kind of discipline Dwight needed. We all needed it. But of course Dwight didn't see it that way because he was too young, just like all of us."

No one had ever taken on Gooden before, and just to make sure Doc understood who the real power broker at Hillsborough was, Reed exercised his authority one more time at the season opener. Doc had won the starting position in right field and asked all his friends, including the girls he was trying to impress, to be at the game. But Gooden was late for homeroom that morning, "maybe by ten seconds," he recalled. Word got back to Reed, who promptly benched Gooden that afternoon.

Dwight's junior year was surprisingly unspectacular, until Youmans and Reed had a falling-out. Youmans asked to leave practice early one afternoon, claiming he had to be home to baby-sit. Reed let the pitcher go but had an intuitive feeling about Youmans's plans. Soon after, Reed left practice, too, and found Youmans playing basketball downtown. He swiftly kicked Youmans off the team and awarded Gooden his spot in the rotation.

"Until then, I'd been a relief pitcher, not really that much of a factor," Gooden said. "If I hadn't gotten that chance . . . I don't know where I would've ended up in baseball." Actually, Youmans was sure Gooden's future in baseball would have been as a third baseman or outfielder. "Dwight was that good of a hitter," he said. "But I gave Dwight his chance. I tell him that all the time."

The following year, Gooden blossomed into an All-Conference pitcher. Although he posted only a 7-4 record, he had a 1.30 ERA, striking out 130 in seventy-five innings. Gooden had played football and basketball growing up, but now his body was developing in a way particularly suited to baseball. He was 6-1, and even though he weighed barely 170 pounds, his arms were unusually long, giving him terrific leverage. With his high leg kick and long-arm delivery, a hitter could believe Gooden's hands were in his face at the end of his delivery, even though Doc was standing sixty feet, six inches away. Adding to the illusion were Gooden's large hands, which could completely hide the ball. The extra millisecond it would take for a hitter to pick up the seams on the ball would be enough to defeat him.

Scouts were convinced Gooden had the talent to become a first-round pick in the 1982 amateur draft, although Doc himself remained unconvinced. "If I got as high as Class A, that would've seemed like the big leagues to me. I would've been happy just getting drafted," Gooden said. Socially, Gooden had managed to stay out of trouble; the incident with the drug dealer had scared him away from cocaine for the time being. He did nothing more than drink the occasional beer with Youmans, Lovelace, Everett, and another friend, Troy Davis, who went on to become a professional boxer.

Ella Gooden was still leaning on her son to pursue an education and she asked him to consider college. In deference to her, Dwight signed a letter of intent to attend the University of Miami, but both he and his father agreed that if he was selected in the first five rounds of the draft, he would skip college and become a pro.

Gooden remembered the day of the draft, being invited to the offices of the *Tampa Tribune* to sit through it. He still had a hard time believing a professional career was ahead of him—even after the Mets made him their first pick and he was the fifth player selected overall in the country. Those selected ahead of Gooden were right-hander Lance McCullers, righty Rich Monteleone, shortstop Shawon Dunston, and another right-hander, Jimmy Jones. Before Gooden agreed to answer any questions from the *Tribune* staff, he first made them call the Mets' offices in New York to verify that he'd been selected because, he later said, "I just couldn't believe it. Even after they hung up the phone and said it was true, a part of me said it was a hoax."

Not to the Mets, who already knew Gooden threw hard enough to make it to the bigs right away. But with only one full year of starting pitching in high school, Gooden was sent to rookie ball. He needed to learn about pitching, and he needed to learn about life away from the cocoon. There were still questions about Gooden's transition into the adult world. Joe McIlvaine, now the Mets' general manager but then the club's scouting director, remembered traveling to Tampa for the signing ceremony and the ensuing celebration party for Dwight. There were friends and family everywhere in the house, enough food to feed the entire neighborhood. It should have been the happiest moment in Gooden's life—had he been there to witness it. "I never forgot that, that in the middle of the party thrown in his behalf, I realized Dwight had left to be with his friends," McIlvaine would say years later. "That struck me as very odd."

That behavior might have been tolerated in Tampa, where everyone—friends, family, teammates, everyone except Billy Reed—treated Gooden deferentially. But after leaving home, Gooden realized the adult world wouldn't always be at his service. That summer, playing rookie-league ball in Kingsport, Gooden suffered a terrible case of homesickness.

"I must've called home one hundred times in the two months that season lasted," Gooden said. "I called home to ask how to wash my clothes, how to cook my food, anything and everything that my mother had done for me my whole life. Finally, I stopped trying. I ate TV dinners every night so I could tell my mom I was at least eating something. I'd say, 'Mom, I cooked some peas tonight.' And she'd say, 'Dwight, that's terrific, how'd you learn to do that?' I didn't tell her TV dinners were what kept me alive. It was so bad that first year, I was very close to just quitting and going back home."

Even the next year, at Class A Lynchburg, in Virginia, Gooden still struggled. He'd spent the winter at home, telling himself it was time to grow up. He learned about laundry and cooking and managing money. Now all he had to do was pitch. But in his first month, Gooden was only 3-3, letting inferior hitters feel comfortable at the plate. Gooden's fastball lacked the anger it possessed in high school. Worst of all, Gooden looked scared on the mound.

It was early May when Gooden found himself in another early-inning jam: bases loaded, no one out, already down 2–0. Pitching coach John Cumberland went to the mound and stared hotly at Gooden. Cumberland was a former major leaguer, and although he won only fifteen games in his six-year career with the Yankees, Giants, Cardinals, and Angels between 1968 and 1974, he understood the difference between a pitcher who had the skill to win and one who had the will.

Cumberland had watched Gooden wallow in doubt for six games already, even though, as he would say years later, "I thought he had the livest arm I'd ever seen on a kid. He should've never lost, not in A-ball." So Cumberland finally decided it was time to awaken Gooden to his failure.

"I wanna ask you a question," Cumberland said, his face inches from the startled Gooden's.

"What's that?" Gooden said innocently.

"*What the fuck is your problem?*" Cumberland shouted. "You're out here, you've got nothing today . . . no balls, nothing. The problem is you don't want to win bad enough. You ain't got it in you. You've got no balls, son."

Gooden started to mouth some response, but Cumberland cut him off. The pitching coach knew if Gooden was ever going to respond, it had to be now, through anger and confrontation and not a dialogue. There was only one way to cut through the years of Doc's pampering, and that was to issue a challenge, right there on the mound, in front of his teammates and the opposing team, with the bases loaded.

"I want you to take the ball and get out of this fucking jam. Do you understand what I'm saying?" Cumberland said. "I want you to show me that you give a shit. I want you to shove the bats right up their butts, and I want you to do it right now. Show me what kind of fucking balls you have because as of right now, I don't think you have any."

And with that, Cumberland turned and walked off the mound. He left Gooden there, holding the ball, an eighteen-year-old at a crossroads. "I'd have to say that was one of the biggest points in my career," Gooden said. "Something in me changed."

He took a deep breath, the kind that stretched the lining of the lungs. And from that point, Gooden's professional career began in earnest. He struck out the side on eleven pitches and didn't allow a run the rest of the game. Gooden went on to win sixteen of his next seventeen decisions and finished the season with a 19-4 record, a 2.50 ERA, and an awesome three hundred strikeouts in just 191 innings. The Mets had seen enough: he was promoted all the way to the big leagues, right from Class A, in 1984. In spring training the next year, the Mets were sure they had inherited the finest right-handed pitcher in franchise history. Dwight Gooden was to become the next Tom Seaver. All he had to do was pitch. All he had to do was walk straight along that unfettered road to Cooperstown.

5

GOIN' DOWN, DOWN, DOWN . . .

THE BACK OF the charter plane is the baseball equivalent of an after-hours bar, where only the socially hip are permitted. There were certain rules the Mets followed in the eighties: the back of the plane was for the drinkers, the card players, and the veterans, in that order. Rookies were banned, as were the born-again God-squaders. The media? Reporters were an endangered species anywhere past the middle of the fuselage.

There were no rules of etiquette in the back of the plane, especially on the longer flights. The greater the amount of alcohol consumed, the uglier the behavior got, which is why the most important rule of all was this: if you were too sensitive to cope with the drunken verbal abuse, then not only was it wise to stay away from the back, even using the rear lavatory was a risk.

The turbine engines of the Mets' TWA charter 727 would roar through the night, but they could never drown out the loudest Mets. And almost always, the player with the toughest, meanest streak when he was drinking was Darryl Strawberry. By 1987, Strawberry was getting deeper into cocaine and, significantly, he remembered, "I was drinking just about every night. I just couldn't stop."

The plane was a comfortable environment for an alcoholic. The liquor supply was endless, and there was never any waiting. All one had to do was ask a flight attendant, who was literally on call throughout the flight. Without a plane full of kids or senior citizens or tourists to serve, there wasn't much else to do except keep pouring the drinks. It was just twenty-five Mets, by themselves, except for four coaches, their manager, and the TV crew, killing time at thirty thousand feet. How much could one drink in that setting? Ron Darling once said, "On a coast-to-coast trip, I saw Frank Viola put away a case of beer like it was nothing."

Viola was happy in alcohol's embrace. Strawberry was not. For all the acts of kindness while sober, something snapped in Strawberry after the fifth or sixth beer. And always, it would manifest itself in teasing. Starting in 1986, Strawberry and Tim Teufel had difficulty with pop-ups in the no-man's-land between second base and right field. Teufel would turn and chase, waiting for Strawberry to call him off. But Strawberry would be distracted by Teufel's pursuit, often backing away at the last instant. Too many times the ball would drop embarrassingly between them, and, after a few weeks, the tension extended beyond the field as well.

His teammates liked Teufel: he was sensible, mature, a gamer, and, above all, he could, it seemed, catch up to any fastball. But take the uniform off him, and Teufel was mild-mannered and definitely not an inner-circle Met. Still, he was accepted enough to earn a nickname, somehow acquiring the moniker "Richard." There was nothing unusual about that since many Mets had pet names: Hernandez was "Mex," Gary Carter was "Kid," Lenny Dykstra was "Nails," Ron Darling was "RJ," and Barry Lyons was "Mattress"—short for "Mattress Head," which was the Mets' good-spirited tribute to his baldness.

How or why Teufel was named Richard didn't have much significance until one day on the plane Strawberry took the nickname to another level of insult.

"Hey, Richard," Strawberry said to Teufel, several rows up. "Hey, Richard, I'm talking to you, Richard. Hey, Richard . . . guess you can't hear me, can you, Richard Head."

It didn't require any great intellectual leap for Teufel to realize Richard Head meant dick head. It wasn't the worst of insults, but there was an edge to Strawberry's voice and an inability—or at least an unwillingness—to know when to stop. The reason for that, teammates said, was Strawberry was drunk.

"Darryl wasn't a lot of fun to be around after he'd had a couple of beers," said first baseman Dave Magadan, who left the Mets via free agency after the 1992 season. "The thing about Darryl was that he always took it too far. It was one thing to get on a guy about his clothes or his haircut, but it was another to get on his family or his ability. I liked Darryl, but I didn't like him when he was drunk. Or when he was hanging around his group of friends on the team."

Teufel was certainly not a member of Strawberry's clique, and Darryl found what he thought was an easy target. The "Richard Head" nickname stuck, although most Mets used the term endearingly. But Strawberry began a back-of-the-plane campaign against Teufel, which, according to teammates, lasted most of the season.

Finally, one day, Teufel decided he'd suffered enough verbal abuse. For all those months, he had listened in quiet rage, never responding to Strawberry, always pretending to forget the insults the next day, when Darryl was sober and wishing the problem would evaporate on its own. But Teufel also understood that as a member of a Met team that took pride in its unrivaled macho quotient, "There comes a point where you have to stand up for your own dignity, where you draw a line in the sand and say, 'Enough.' Over the course of a career, you'll get challenged, whether it's by a pitcher knocking you down or, sometimes, a teammate. Either way, your integrity is what's being challenged, who you are as a person, and it's up to you to do something about it."

According to teammates, Teufel got up from his seat, turned on Strawberry, and, still several rows apart, started shouting: "I'm tired of listening to you, I've had it." He took several steps toward Darryl, who for the moment was so startled he didn't respond. Several Mets stepped in between them, and, luckily for Teufel, no punches were ever thrown. The bigger, stronger, and more volatile Strawberry would have made short work out of the second baseman. But that wasn't the point. One veteran pitcher said, "What really mattered is that Timmy had the balls to stand up to Straw and say, 'No more.' I swear to God, something changed in Teufel from that day forward. He was a different guy—not only in the clubhouse but on the field, too. He hit better, he played better defense. All around the league, players were saying, 'What the hell came over Teufel?' It's like he became a man."

The truth was that Teufel and Strawberry liked each other, if not before the incident on the plane, then certainly afterward. Darryl came to respect the combative side in his second baseman, his willingness to stand up to a bigger, stronger foe, and made a point of always being respectful to Teufel's family when they visited Shea Stadium.

"That was part of Darryl's charm, the way he could get people to like him instantly," said Teufel, who now works in San Diego as a financial consultant. "What impressed me was the way he treated my father, who was sixty-eight years old and a real old-school type of guy. But Darryl was cordial to him, and I've never forgotten that. The sad part is the way Darryl could act when he was clearheaded, it made the way he acted drunk that much harder to accept. In his heart, Straw was really a good guy."

But alcohol—not to mention amphetamines—changed Strawberry in a way that only his closest friends could tolerate. And even that wasn't always true. Gooden said, "Back in eighty-six and eighty-seven, when Darryl was using amphetamines a lot, he was a hostile, angry guy. I remember he used to come to the park looking for a fight. He'd say to Mitch [Kevin Mitchell], 'Come on, let's fuck somebody up today.'"

One of Strawberry's targets in 1986 was Cincinnati left-hander Tom Browning, whom Darryl disliked "for no real reason," according to Teufel. "I don't know what he had against the guy, but both Darryl and Lenny [Dykstra] couldn't stand him. They didn't even like the way Browning looked." For years, it seemed, Strawberry had been looking for a reason to fight Browning, and he finally got his chance when Browning and Teufel were involved in an altercation.

Teufel was at the plate, and as Browning began his windup, the second baseman stepped out of the batter's box. Browning was charged with a balk, and Pete Rose, who was managing the Reds at the time, charged out of the dugout to argue the call. As Rose was powerless to reverse a balk call, he went to the mound and instructed Browning to hit Teufel with his next pitch. It was a fastball, and it caught Teufel on the ribs.

"There was no question it was intentional," Teufel said. "I was on the ground, feeling pretty lousy, but out of the corner of my eye, I saw Darryl charging out of the dugout, going right at Browning. I said, 'Uh-oh, here we go.' All hell broke loose." The incident was remembered not only for Strawberry's intervention but for the devastating right cross that Mets infielder Ray Knight ultimately landed on Eric Davis's jaw. For all his power and fury, not even Strawberry would have been a match for Knight, at least not in boxing. A former Golden Gloves champ, Knight heard after the Reds' brawl that the muscular Dave Parker was ready to take him on the next day if there were any more Reds that Knight wanted to fight. "I'll be at the batting cage, he knows where to find me," Parker said menacingly.

The next day came, and Knight made a point of walking slowly by the batting cage, obviously ready for whatever Parker had in mind. The huge, muscular Reds outfielder said nothing, stared straight ahead, choosing not to provoke an opponent who was so unafraid. That could explain why Strawberry got along so well with Knight until the infielder left the Mets after the 1986 World Series. As Gooden put it, "Darryl liked anyone who was strong enough to take what he dished out. Most of the time, he was just testing guys to see how far they could be pushed. It told him what kind of guts they really had."

Not even Gooden was immune from Strawberry's rage. On the way to Boston for game three of the 1986 Series, the two had an altercation that began when Gooden demanded a drink from a flight attendant. "I knew she was busy, but I asked two or three times, and she still didn't seem to have time for me, so I said, 'What's the problem here?' " Gooden recalled. "Out of nowhere, Straw starts getting on my case, telling me, 'Man, you can't be talking to people like that.' He was real strong about it, like he was challenging me. So I said, 'Fuck you, don't be talking to me like that.' Next thing I know we were both standing up, and a couple of guys had to come between us. We laughed about it later. The thing about Darryl was, you could make fun of him as much as you wanted. He could take it. He just wanted to see how much you could take."

But when Strawberry sensed weakness, he exploited it mercilessly. Perhaps the worst verbal lashing he ever doled out was to left-hander Gene Walter, a shy journeyman reliever who played with the Mets in 1987 and 1988. Strawberry rode Walter so hard, Magadan said, "even the guys who usually laughed at all Darryl's jokes, guys like Mex and Ronnie Darling and Doc, who made Darryl think he was funny, even they got quiet. It was awful. I've never felt so sorry for a player than I did for Gene. Darryl was getting on him about his lack of control—he had almost thrown the ball to the backstop on an intentional walk that day. He was new to New York and not a very vocal guy on top of that. He just took it."

In retrospect, Strawberry knew there was no defending or rationalizing his behavior, especially when he was drunk. "I was just an unhappy guy who didn't know any better," Darryl said. "Drinking was the only way I knew how to deal with pressure. It's what allowed me to escape from myself, and I realize now there were a lot of things I said that I should've never said. I know I hurt a lot of people."

If the Mets players were so aware of Strawberry's troubles, then where was Met management? If anyone was in a position to intervene, it was Davey Johnson, who was responsible for the conduct of his players and the climate in his clubhouse. Generally, Johnson liked to delegate authority to his coaches;

for instance, Buddy Harrelson was usually in charge of clearing out the players' lounge when too many Mets disappeared from the dugout in the middle of a game. But Davey knew Strawberry was his domain.

He had managed Strawberry for only a month at Triple-A in 1983 before the desperate Mets summoned the still raw right fielder. Ever since that day, Johnson said, "I felt kind of sorry for Darryl. He was overwhelmed from the beginning. In my opinion they should've kept Darryl at Triple-A all year. Shoot, the Mets still finished last with him." Strawberry struck out three times in his debut, overmatched by the magical change-up of Reds right-hander Mario Soto. Darryl's mother, Ruby, watched from the stands and said, "I saw this look in Darryl's eyes that day, and I knew right away the pressure was getting to him."

But no matter how aware Johnson was of Strawberry's oppressive surroundings, he many times fought the urge to confront Strawberry, especially when his drinking and back-of-the-plane behavior were excessive. "I have to admit, there were times I heard Darryl getting on me, for not hitting him cleanup, or for not using Mookie [Wilson] instead of Lenny, that I pretended not to hear what was going on," Johnson said. "The truth is, if I'd gone to the back of the plane, I'm sure I would've fought him, and I might've killed him. That's how angry I was at times. But I let it go, I let it go because I had no doubt that if there was an incident, it would've ended up on the back page of the *Post* or *Daily News,* and then where would we be? Darryl was a sensitive guy, and I'm not sure he would've benefitted from the negative publicity. At least that's what I told myself at the time.

"Now . . . I don't know. Sometimes I blame myself for not doing more for Darryl. Maybe it would've woken him up if his manager, his father figure, had gotten in his face and maybe beaten the hell out of him. I knew Darryl wasn't living up to the example of a star athlete. I knew he was having his problems at home and bringing them to the ballpark. I knew he was drinking. I told him, so many times, 'Darryl, there are three vices that'll destroy your career: sex, drinking, and not enough sleep. At least pick one, but not all three.' And he'd say, 'I agree.' So I'd say, 'What can I do to help?' And Straw would just say he had it under control. And he'd walk out of my office, and the problem just kept getting worse. I just wish I'd done more."

Actually, Johnson was half hoping his two captains, Keith Hernandez and Gary Carter, would be able to penetrate Strawberry's wall of denial. But there were problems in that tack, too. Hernandez was leading just as active a nightlife as Strawberry, and Carter was so deep into his born-again Christianity he could never relate to Darryl or his lifestyle. "I heard a tremendous amount of abuse from Darryl, mostly about the way I lived my life," said Carter, who retired in 1992 and now broadcasts Florida Marlins games. "He'd get a few beers in him, and by the time we reached our destination he was pretty well snockered. Then he'd start on me, telling me, 'Kid, you don't ever go out. You don't do anything with your life, do you?' I wanted to shut him up because it was so obnoxious, so abusive. But it really wasn't worth it. For one thing, I really felt sorry for Darryl more than anything else; he was such a mixed-up guy. And let's be honest, Darryl was six-six, carved out of stone. If he really wanted to, he could've killed a man. I'd go to Mex and say, 'Can't you do anything about Darryl?' And Keith would say, 'I can't do anything, he won't listen to me. Why don't you talk to him.' I tried, we all tried. But it didn't really seem to get through to him at the time."

That's because, by 1987, as his drinking and amphetamine use accelerated—not to mention his cocaine use, which was now growing more regular—Strawberry's marriage was also dissolving. He had married Lisa Andrews in January 1985, almost two years after having met her at a Lakers game at the Forum in Los Angeles. The couple began fighting even before they were married, one usually accusing the other of infidelity.

"A few weeks before the wedding, Darryl and Lisa stopped talking to each other altogether," said Strawberry's agent Richie Bry. "It finally got so bad, I said to him, 'Darryl, you better give this thing a second thought.' He was so immature he said, 'What about all the invitations?' I guess they'd sent out more than three hundred, but I said, 'So you'll be a little embarrassed for a couple of weeks. That's nothing compared to the alternative.' " Strawberry listened politely to Bry's counsel but went ahead with the marriage anyway. Bry, in fact, wrote a check for half the costs out of his own pocket.

Strawberry also heard complaints from his mother, who took an instant dislike to her highly assertive future daughter-in-law. "In my opinion, Darryl got married far too young, and I told him that," Ruby said. "Here he was, just a year or two in the major leagues, and he was making a choice for a lifetime. He still hadn't learned how to be an adult yet, so how could Darryl have been ready to be a husband or a father? I hated to say I told you so, but I could see problems coming."

Friends say money was at the core of the Strawberrys' conflict. Lisa liked to live comfortably, but once Darryl signed a six-year contract worth $7.2 million, their finances soon spun out of control. Bry had referred Strawberry to a respected St. Louis–based financial planner, Kathy Lintz, since the agent had deferred much of Darryl's salary until after the ball-player's retirement. The deal called for Strawberry to receive

$300,000 a year for thirty years as soon as his playing days were over. But Lintz soon discovered the Strawberrys were unable—or unwilling—to control their spending. "Darryl always treated me with the utmost respect and courtesy, but I never could get through to him," said Lintz. "I mean, it wasn't unusual for us to receive twenty thousand dollars a month in American Express bills. We tried pie charts, diagrams, tables . . . everything. But they had mortgages on two homes, several cars, and Darryl even wanted to put some of his siblings on the payroll because they couldn't find work. Sooner or later, that adds up." After a while, Lintz realized her warnings were being met with increasing annoyance, and finally her phone calls went unreturned altogether.

It wasn't long before Strawberry dipped into his deferred income, but no matter how much extra cash he infused his marriage with—including money from card-show appearances, which ultimately led to criminal prosecution by the IRS—there was no calming the tension within his marriage. "You could just tell the days Darryl had just had a fight at home," said trainer Steve Garland. One day in 1985, Strawberry and Gooden were riding together to Shea Stadium from their homes in Port Washington, Long Island, and it was clear to Gooden that his friend had just been arguing with Lisa. He hardly said a word to Gooden, and it wasn't until they reached the players' entrance that Strawberry finally turned to him and said, "Take me back home. I ain't finished with her yet." Gooden turned around and drove all the way back to Long Island.

Many of the problems in the Strawberry household were generated by money, but they were exacerbated by his drinking and drug use. "I admit, I used to smack Lisa around all the time. It was nothing that I was proud of—then or now. Anytime you see a case of domestic violence, believe me, it comes from drinking and using. What do you think the O.J. thing was about? Those pictures of Nicole, her eyes black-ened . . . God, tell me that wasn't about using," Strawberry said. "But Lisa used to hit me, too. She thought she was really tough. She'd talk crazy to me, and sometimes, you know, I just didn't want to hear it. So I hit her. It was part of a vicious cycle on my side: drinking and drugging and coming home and taking it out on my wife. It wasn't until a few years later that I realized that I was acting the same way that my father used to. And I hated that."

Lisa Strawberry claimed that by citing drinking and drugs as an excuse for domestic violence, Strawberry was guilty of "a cover-up; it was an excuse." She also said that New York's cul-ture of hero worship led Strawberry to believe that "he could do no wrong. He was all of New York's savior. People thought maybe I provoked him to hit me."

The 1987 season was a crossroads for Strawberry, as it was for many Mets. They had just won the World Series from the Red Sox, but that winter, Knight left as a free agent, signing with the Orioles. Kevin Mitchell was exported, too, as the front office believed he was taking Strawberry and Gooden down. But in retrospect, Mitchell wasn't the problem at all, or, at least, his disappearance had no effect on the downward spiral of his two teammates. Gooden began experimenting with cocaine in earnest and would test positive for the drug in April. Strawberry and Lisa separated, and she filed for an order of protection in January. Although they reconciled eight months later, Strawberry spent much of the '87 season out after games, partying with teammates and friends.

There wasn't a sports editor in New York City who didn't, at any one point or another during the year, receive an anonymous tip that Strawberry was using cocaine. Actually, rumors had enveloped both Strawberry and Gooden starting in 1986, when they were allegedly seen in bars all over Long Island and New York cops whispered they knew the times and places the Mets were using. Gooden's fall to coke in early 1987 only intensified the focus on Strawberry, and while outsiders had no real proof, reporters who covered the Mets sensed the increasing polarity of Darryl's mood swings. In a mere seven-day span in June of 1987, Strawberry overslept twice, each time requiring the assistance of a teammate to get him to the park, where he was fined and benched by Davey Johnson, and in one game he charged the mound after nearly being hit by a pitch. Yet Strawberry continued to sign autographs for kids and treat fans warmly while publicly denying drugs were his problem. Even from the outset, when Gooden tested positive in spring training, Strawberry said, "I could've easily gotten involved with that stuff, but I didn't." That was a lie, Strawberry admitted years later. And who knew better than Gooden himself?

How easy it would have been for Gooden to point a finger at the "twelve or thirteen guys" on the team who he said were using drugs. But he wouldn't do that, he said, "because that's not the way I was, or am. I wanted to at least try to help Darryl, but what reason did he have to listen to me? I had my own problems. I was in the same boat with him. We were both using drugs."

Still, the two players were drifting apart as friends. Strawberry was conspicuously absent from Gooden's wedding in 1986, choosing to remain in Los Angeles for a sporting-goods appearance with Eric Davis. Although Doc and Darryl were still linked in fans' minds, the truth was, "We pretty much stopped hanging out together," Gooden said. "Especially after he got married. We went our separate ways."

That was particularly true after night games during road trips, when Strawberry would take to bars and clubs with Ron Darling and Kevin Elster and, later, David Cone. Gooden was less of a social butterfly; in fact, it was rare when he was seen at all in the bars on the road. It was that lifestyle that Strawberry believed took him down. "It wasn't one thing, it was everything—the drinking, the women who hung around, just the whole atmosphere," he said. "And I couldn't get away from it. I had no idea how to get my life back. It was always the same habit after games: go out, get drunk, chase after women, do some drugs, come to the park the next day feeling like you're dead."

His brother Michael, a former Los Angeles police officer, told the *L.A. Times,* "I knew Darryl had problems when I would visit him in New York. He was separated from his wife, so he would go out with his friends all night. I tried to go out with them once during the winter in Los Angeles, and I couldn't keep up. The big cars, the money, the partying, it was too much for me."

Under the major-league drug policy in force in the eighties, no team could compel a player to take a drug test. Unless Strawberry volunteered, he was safe. But he had no doubt the Met front office was aware of the problem. "I really believe Frank Cashen might've known, but he didn't do anything about it," Strawberry said. The former general manager, who retired after the 1991 season, declined to respond to Strawberry's remark, although a current Met official said Strawberry's claim was "nonsense."

As Strawberry's money situation worsened, he demanded the Mets renegotiate his contract in 1987. The club refused, and Strawberry walked out of spring training. It was Johnson who personally pleaded with Cashen to make a onetime exception for Darryl, telling the executive, "It's obvious this guy is in trouble." But Cashen was unwilling to bend, and Strawberry believed that was the beginning of the end of his love affair with the Mets. He was also having problems within the clubhouse. He skipped a critical night game against the Cardinals, blaming a virus, although earlier in the day he was recording a rap song. It was then that Wally Backman remarked, "No one I know gets sick twenty-five times a year." To that, Strawberry said, "I'll bust that little redneck in the face."

It was an unusually violent reaction, even by Strawberry's standards. And it was the first time Darryl had ever played the race card. He had had his private suspicions about the different treatment accorded black athletes in New York—he wondered, for instance, why Kevin McReynolds was treated so much more benevolently by the public, despite the left fielder's aloof, almost indifferent playing style. Strawberry was no racist, but to call Backman a redneck set off an alarm. At least it did for Backman.

"I could never understand what that was all about," said Backman, who was traded to the Twins in 1988, retired in 1993, and now lives in Oregon. "The only thing I could imagine that Darryl had against me is that I was really, really close friends with Dwight. Who knows, maybe Straw was jealous of that. I was never sure. But he shouldn't have had anything against me."

Maybe it was that as a member of Strawberry's inner circle, Backman had less tolerance for Strawberry's failures. The little second baseman always prided himself on being brutally honest—and, in fact, said his one-year tenure with the Twins in 1989 was doomed from the moment he realized, "They were way too straitlaced for me. First time I said 'fuck' they looked at me like I was from another planet." So Backman was equally candid about his use of cocaine in his Met days. "Yeah, I partied," he said. "But I did it socially, I never had a problem with drugs. I knew when to shut it down. Some guys didn't."

One of them, in Backman's opinion, was Strawberry. Backman rejected Darryl's contention that his addiction in the eighties was alcohol. "That's a line of shit. I was there. I saw what Darryl's problem was," he said. "Darryl just couldn't stay away from the stuff. There's no doubt in my mind he had a real problem . . . but look, he deserves a second chance, like anyone else. If he has to say drinking was the problem, to get his head on straight, then let him say it. Drinking was sure part of it. But not the whole thing."

Not every Met had such a close-up look at Strawberry's darker side. Of course, the rumors flew throughout the clubhouse, but only a few Mets actually witnessed his drug use. Equipment manager Charlie Samuels said, "I never saw any evidence that Darryl was using drugs, never saw him show up at the park high, never saw drugs in his locker, never had any idea that was going on. We all knew Darryl was having problems with Lisa. He just went for the wrong release."

"Looking back, Darryl wasn't very obvious about it," said Steve Garland. "I mean, I didn't think he was any different than Lenny or Mex. I thought he was just another guy who liked to party. He'd rarely show up at the park early, and he looked bad, but I attributed it to drinking."

By 1989, Strawberry had switched agents, going from Bry to the L.A.-based Eric Goldschmidt, and he was a year away from switching teams, too. Goldschmidt lured Strawberry away by telling him Bry had undersold him for years. That pitch was re-inforced by Darryl's buddy Eric Davis, another Goldschmidt client and a devotee. Goldschmidt was barely 5-7, baby-faced and often dressed in nonthreatening attire like jeans and tennis sneakers. But he had the negotiating edge of a shark, and the Mets soon came to loathe him. In fact, some Met officials say it was having to deal with Goldschmidt that drove Cashen into retirement. The little general manager came from a purer, simpler era in baseball, when agents didn't have egos—or paychecks—as large as some of the players'. At least the Mets considered Bry an honorable man. But Bry was no match for Goldschmidt's seduction, which aimed directly at Darryl's thirst for cash. "Not that I ever disliked Richie or anything, but I honestly thought Eric could get me a better deal," Strawberry said.

Bry resented Goldschmidt deeply for stealing Strawberry. "Darryl was easy prey because he had no money," his former agent said. "It's easy to say to a guy it's the agent's fault. But that's the way Goldschmidt did business. He didn't get his clients in the minor leagues and work his way up with them, which is the way you're supposed to do it in this industry. He would just take them from other agents. I was hearing about Goldschmidt for about a year before Darryl left me. People were saying, 'Watch out,' so I confronted Darryl, and he told me, 'Don't worry, there's no way I would leave you.' Eventually, he did."

Bry was right about Strawberry's finances: Darryl was more desperate than ever for cash, even asking teammates for money. After the end of their professional relationship, Bry said, "Darryl's marriage to Lisa became a contest of who could outspend the other." Still, the Mets refused to renegotiate Strawberry's contract, which was to expire after the 1990 season, or even to offer him an extension.

Clearly, the front office was concerned about Strawberry's drinking and his off-the-field behavior. In the spring of '89, he and Keith Hernandez engaged in the now infamous fistfight during Picture Day—a public relations nightmare, considering it took place while TV cameras were rolling. What began as a minor spat—Strawberry refused to stand next to Hernandez in the team lineup—exploded into a much larger dispute. Strawberry had been told that Hernandez had campaigned against him the previous season, telling writers that Kevin McReynolds, and not Darryl, deserved the Most Valuable Player Award. As it turned out, neither player won, as the Dodgers' Kirk Gibson was the top vote getter. But who knows how many votes Strawberry lost because of Hernandez's comments?

It was the saddest betrayal, because Strawberry spent so many years admiring Hernandez. Like Jimmy Frey and Davey Johnson before him, Hernandez was just another father figure in Darryl's life, although this one led a far more complicated and troubled life. By his own admission, Hernandez had used cocaine in the eighties. He, too, had endured domestic troubles during a bitter divorce and, even after all that, as Met captain, smoked and drank and wasn't above taking on his teammates, off the record, with the press. But there was something about Hernandez that was impossible to dislike: his ability to make the players around him compete at a higher level.

Right-hander Ed Lynch, who is now the general manager of the Chicago Cubs, said, "Keith was so intense, it was like he was insane on the field. He wouldn't think twice about standing on the top step of the dugout and calling the opposing pitcher a cunt if he happened to get him out with a change-up. I mean, he would stand there and shout it at the top of his lungs. Players today don't do that. They're a much different breed. Mex is why we were so damned tough."

But as much as a to-the-core Met as he was, Hernandez couldn't stop criticizing Strawberry. Charlie Samuels said, "I always sensed this great tension between them. It never seemed to go away." Hernandez's skills were declining by 1989, and it was clear that both he and Gary Carter were through in New York. Even Hernandez's critics seemed saddened by his unraveling because in his prime in the early to mid-eighties no one was tougher to strike out with men in scoring position than Hernandez. His ability to read pitchers' minds, to outguess them in the most critical situations, was what drove the Mets. "Keith and Gary took the heat off everyone," Davey Johnson said. If nothing else, though, losing Hernandez and Carter should have automatically anointed Strawberry and Gooden as the Mets' newest front men, but Gooden had lost something magical off his fastball and Strawberry, still suffering the P.R. fallout from his fight with Hernandez, suffered the worst year of his career, hitting just .225 with twenty-nine homers and seventy-seven RBIs. Although the Mets finished second, Johnson nearly lost his job, as the club failed to win ninety games for the first time since he became manager in 1984. After the season, both Hernandez and Carter moved on, and although Carter enjoyed three more years before retiring, Hernandez quickly disappeared from the baseball community. He signed a two-year deal with the Indians that winter but played only forty-three games in 1990 before a back injury forced his retirement.

Hernandez is still a fixture in New York's social scene today, still visible at Elaine's, still getting his name in boldface in the society pages. But one Met official, a friend, voices concern that Hernandez has yet to begin, or even find, his after-baseball life. "The problem is that Keith refuses to believe nineteen eighty-five has come and gone. We try to tell him, 'Keith, find something to do,' " the friend says. At times, he still acts like the Met captain of old. When *Sports*

Illustrated ran a cover story in February 1995 detailing the rise and fall of the Mets, chronicling Strawberry's and Gooden's drug problems, it was Hernandez who wrote a letter to the editor the next week. He harshly criticized both players for daring to soil the Mets' name. Yet, several months later, when Hernandez was at Yankee Stadium for a guest appearance as a color commentator, he walked into the Yankee clubhouse, sought out Strawberry, and hugged him. Darryl, as always, forgave. He hugged Hernandez right back.

THE DEPARTURE OF another Met left a gaping hole in Darryl's landscape in 1990. Davey Johnson was fired only forty-two games into the season, and it was Strawberry who said he would leave the Mets, too, as a free agent, after the season. "I loved that man. He deserves better than this," Darryl said, meaning it. Strawberry blamed Frank Cashen for Davey's demise, although there were teammates who held Strawberry accountable as well, since he didn't play in the final few games of the '89 season. "That ticked off a lot of guys," Magadan said. "It got to the point where we were sick of Darryl always being injured or tired or whatever. Darryl did the same thing at the end of the nineteen ninety season. At that time of the year, if you're in a pennant race, if you can walk, you can play. I know Darryl had a bad back, but it's still something I never forgot."

Actually, 1990 was an important crossroads in Strawberry's life. The Mets announced that Strawberry was seeking help for alcoholism, but that was just an escape hatch to avoid prosecution from his January domestic-violence arrest. Incredibly, Strawberry convinced Smithers officials that he indeed limited his addiction to drinking. "I never bothered to tell them about the drugs," he said. "The truth is that I was still in denial; I hadn't faced up to the fact that I was an addict. I tried to separate the drinking from the drugging, but it was only later that I figured out it was all part of the same thing. But back in nineteen ninety, I wasn't ready yet."

Strawberry finished out the 1990 season with a career-high 108 RBIs, as well as thirty-seven homers and a .277 average. But just as it had the year before, the club collapsed in September. The only difference is that Buddy Harrelson was the victim, instead of Davey Johnson, and in less than two years, the Mets of the eighties, the Golden Era Mets, would be scattered to the wind, existing only in the memory banks of their fans. Strawberry left for Los Angeles, Backman and Dykstra were already gone, Ron Darling was traded in 1991 to the Expos and then to the A's. David Cone awaited a similar fate in 1992, going to the Blue Jays. New general manager Al Harazin brought with him a new manager in Jeff Torborg for 1992, a new supply of out-of-town talent in Bobby Bonilla, Eddie Murray, and Vince Coleman—and just like that, the old Mets were gone. For Strawberry, returning to L.A. made all the sense in the world, especially since the Dodgers had awarded him a five-year contract for $20.25 million. Cashen had offered Darryl four years for $16 million and seemed stoic when Strawberry exercised the only option he had, which was to leave. "We'll see now if it was a good move [by the Dodgers] by the end of the contract," Cashen said.

But Dodgers general manager Fred Claire said, "Our expectations were big. Darryl was at an age [twenty-eight] where he should've been reaching the peak of his career. We had some younger players who were on the way, guys like Eric Karros and Mike Piazza and Raul Mondesi, and we believed Darryl would be the bridge to that younger generation of Dodgers."

Strawberry struggled in his first year, but he finished strong. With a .265 average, twenty-eight home runs, and ninety-nine RBIs, he appeared to have proven Cashen wrong. More important, Strawberry said, "For the first time in a long, long time, I cleaned myself up. I stopped the drinking and definitely stopped using coke. Everything looked good for me from that point on." Darryl was returning to his former neighborhood, but he had vowed to make a clean break. At first, that promise seemed to be true. Strawberry learned that a former friend and teammate at Crenshaw High School had been arrested for allegedly murdering his mother and was on trial. The friend asked that Strawberry attend the court sessions as a show of support, but Darryl said no, sending word through his brother Mike, who recalled, "He couldn't do anything for the guy. Darryl realized that part of his life was over, that there wasn't anything he could do for the guy. He had to move on."

It's possible Strawberry's life path would have been different had it not been for a devastating back injury in 1992. The previous year, he had discovered born-again Christianity, although that conversion was met with skepticism in the Dodger clubhouse. There, Strawberry was reunited with Gary Carter, who said, "It almost seemed like a front for Darryl, to be saying those things about Christ. Maybe he did change, I don't really know. But there were plenty of times me and [teammate and fellow Christian] Brett Butler would invite Darryl to breakfast, just to talk about Christ, and he would never show up. He'd say, 'Sure, sure I'll be there,' and then he never would. That was vintage Darryl, eager to please, looking for acceptance, but not always ready for commitment."

Whatever positive energy Christianity may have offered Strawberry, it was negated by the back injury, which limited him to just seventy-five games over the '92 and '93 seasons. In addition, his marriage to Lisa was again dissolving, this time for good. The breakup was finalized on October 15, 1993, and Lisa was granted the couple's home in Encino, a 1991 BMW 750i, a 1989 Porsche 928, a 1991 Mercedes SL, $300,000 in cash, $95,000 in attorney's fees, $50,000 in spousal support, and $30,000 in child support for Darryl junior and Diamond Nicole. Much of Lisa's case in divorce court rested on the proclamation that she knew Darryl was using drugs during the marriage and that she put up with it. Strawberry denied that, saying, "She only claims she knew to get more money out of me. That's what it was all about from the start—money. She never said she knew about the drugs when it was going on."

So, by 1992, Strawberry said, "I was back to using coke, and this time, I was doing it three or four times a week. It started with drinking because I was depressed that my marriage was breaking up and how ugly it got. But the drinking led me right back to coke. I would go off on different runs. I was aware that I was taking myself down, but I just couldn't stop it. I was trying to relieve the pain and the depression. I was home in L.A., but I couldn't do anything to help the Dodgers. This was my dream, and it was turning out like a nightmare."

That disappointment of the '92 season was compounded by the fact that Eric Davis, his boyhood friend, had also returned home. Davis came to the Dodgers from the Reds, and the expectations were so high, Fred Claire said, "It was almost too much for any two young men to bear." But Los Angeles was desperate for positive karma, especially in the wake of the Rodney King beating. What better way for the community to feel better about itself than to see two of its own, Strawberry and Davis, lead the Dodgers to a pennant?

In his best years in Cincinnati, between 1986 and 1990, Davis hit 148 homers, twice reached 100 RBIs, and even stole fifty bases one of those summers. He might not have had Strawberry's overwhelming power, but he hit for a higher average, was a better base stealer, and was still capable of taking any pitcher deep. But Davis had never been the same outfielder since injuring his kidneys in the 1990 World Series against the A's, and injuries continued to plague him in Los Angeles as well.

While Strawberry headed for the surgeon's knife, Davis appeared in only seventy-six games in 1992. "I think Darryl and I were in the same lineup only twenty times or something. It was pretty sad," Davis said wistfully. "I could live with it because I gave the Dodgers everything I had. There was nothing for me to be ashamed of. But Darryl took it a lot harder. Remember, this is the man who wanted the weight of the world on his shoulders. He's always wanted the attention, he became a master of the challenge. It was always true that Darryl did his best when people were against him. That's because he was a great athlete. Now, all of a sudden, his body broke down. Darryl had no idea how to handle it. He wanted to please all of Los Angeles, and now he couldn't."

There were rumors throughout the National League, some of which reached the Met clubhouse, that Strawberry's drug habit had gone from cocaine to crack. He denied the charge. "I never used it. Ever," he said. "There are too many signs that would've been dead giveaways if I had. Professional athletes cannot use crack and not have it show in their performance. Everyone knows what that drug does to people. If I was on crack, I would've been too messed up to even step on the field."

"If Darryl really was on crack, he would've been wearing the same clothes for three or four days, no shower, no food, that type of stuff. That never happened," Davis said. "To be honest, I'm not even sure Darryl had a drug problem. Or at least, if he did, I've seen a lot worse than his."

It was around this time that *Darryl!*, Strawberry's ghost-written autobiography, in which he suggested that Gooden had been high during the 1986 season, and even pitched during the World Series under the influence of coke, was published. Gooden denied it then and continues to do so today. "I didn't start using drugs until after the season," he says. But in spring training of 1992, not long after the book had been released, Gooden confronted Strawberry when the Mets played the Dodgers in Vero Beach.

"Straw, what're you saying that stuff about me for? You know I could bury you if I wanted," Gooden said.

"Doc, I had no idea that was in the book," Strawberry replied. "Some of the stuff that was in there I didn't read before it was published." Gooden grudgingly accepted the explanation, although he wasn't entirely satisfied with it. Nevertheless, Doc never mentioned it again, and the story quietly faded away after a day or two.

There were more pressing problems ahead for Strawberry, though. After batting just .225 with five homers and twenty-five RBIs in 1992, Strawberry had back surgery in September of '92, then obviously returned far too soon. On and off the disabled list for most of the next summer, Strawberry totaled just one hundred at-bats in 1993 and saw his average fall to an embarrassing .140. Even more disturbing was the observation of boyhood friend and former major leaguer Chris Brown, who in 1993 said, "The bad element has been around Strawberry, and it's worked against him."

Even in 1992, the Dodgers were sensing their experiment was failing. Carter said, "They couldn't wait to get rid of Darryl." The front office finally got its chance before the 1994 season. Despite the fact that Strawberry had rehabilitated his back, was hitting the ball well in spring training, and had otherwise conducted himself professionally, his demons swallowed him up one last time in Los Angeles.

What precipitated his final fall to cocaine was a face-to-face meeting with Tommy Lasorda in the Dodger manager's office. Through most of the 1991 season, Lasorda had been supportive of Darryl. But his enthusiasm waned in 1992 and 1993 as Strawberry went into his funk. Several times Lasorda had begged the Dodger front office to release Strawberry, but Claire still had too much money invested in the outfielder, and, up to that point, there was no way the Dodgers could void Strawberry's contract. But they certainly combed the fine print, wondering how many incidents it would take for Darryl to self-destruct entirely.

In April of 1993, at home in Los Angeles, Strawberry happened upon a homeless couple while grocery shopping at a local supermarket. He had his son with him and was feeling in a benevolent mood. The couple, a youngish-looking man and woman, asked Darryl for money. He reached into his wallet and produced a twenty-dollar bill.

"You guys aren't gonna spend this money on getting high, are you? You have any place to stay?" Strawberry recalled asking.

"No, we're on the street. We move from place to place," the woman said.

"Well, let me help you find a hotel or something," Strawberry said. He took his son home and, a few minutes later, returned to the market and asked the couple to get in his car.

Strawberry drove them to a Motel Six, took a room in his name, and checked the man and woman in. When they got to the room, according to Strawberry, "The guy attacked me. It was out of the blue, all of a sudden, he's punching me in the head, the face . . . for no reason at all. Here I was trying to help two people that I was feeling sorry for, even though they were obviously high. I just wanted to know my money wasn't going to be used for drugs. So the guy goes off on me, and yeah, I had to defend myself. Later, the woman apologized: she said he always did that when he was high, attacking people who tried to help them out. I learned my lesson."

Not entirely. In June of that same year, Strawberry was fined one day's pay, almost $20,000, for arriving at Dodger Stadium after the start of a game and for missing a rehabilitation assignment. Claire made a point of announcing Strawberry's violation and subsequent penalty to the press, in part, he said, because "I wanted Darryl to know we weren't going to cover up for him." In September, he was arrested for striking his girlfriend and future wife, Charisse Simon. Strawberry was fortunate no charges were ever brought because the Dodgers would have certainly been ready to set him free had he been prosecuted. And in March of 1994, a month before his final break with the Dodgers, Strawberry learned he was under investigation by the IRS for tax fraud.

Lasorda decided to cut through the layers of Strawberry's crises with a simple and forceful message. He called the outfielder into his office just before the Dodgers were to play the California Angels in Los Angeles, the final exhibition game before Opening Day. Lasorda said, "You've got to get going this year. We're depending on you. We're paying you a lot of money."

Something sank inside Strawberry. "I just couldn't stand Lasorda anymore," he said. "He wasn't my friend, he was just a two-faced guy. Didn't he understand I didn't play baseball for money? I played because I loved the game. I just didn't want to hear him anymore. I got the feeling he was jealous of me for some reason. I know he had his own problems. I didn't even want to go to the games."

Even considering his simmering resentment toward Lasorda, Strawberry surprised many with his sudden disappearance. "I didn't think there was anything that wrong that would push Darryl over the edge like that," teammate Eric Davis said. "At least he didn't say anything to me about it beforehand. I guess something inside of Straw just had it."

"In the entire spring training, Darryl seemed to be a model citizen. He didn't seem to have a problem with Tommy," said Ken Daley, who covered the Dodgers for the Los Angeles *Daily News.* "The timing of it seemed kind of odd, just because it was so unexpected."

Strawberry walked out of Lasorda's office and disappeared into the night. He never made it to Dodger Stadium the next day, and it wasn't until weeks later that Claire heard rumors that Strawberry had spent the day at a crack house. To this day, the general manager says, "I still haven't heard a satisfactory explanation as to Darryl's whereabouts."

Strawberry was seen later that night at a nightclub with Reggie Williams, although they parted ways around midnight. Strawberry would only say he had spent the next afternoon "at a friend's house." Charisse, now his wife, couldn't find him. Nor could Darryl's mother. When the Dodgers started making phone calls, they realized Strawberry had, indeed, disappeared. It wasn't until that evening that Darryl finally called Claire and said, "Don't worry, I'm okay, everything is fine." Two years of frustration finally bubbled to the surface, as Claire nearly shouted into the phone, "No, Darryl, everything is not fine. You get yourself together, get your agent, your attorney, your family members, anybody you think you'll need, and you be in my office tomorrow morning at nine A.M." And that marked the beginning of the end of Strawberry's career as a Dodger.

The next day, Strawberry arrived with his family and his lawyer, Robert Shapiro, who was then only two months away from his first meeting with O. J. Simpson. It was Shapiro who suggested to Strawberry that he finally confess his drug problem to his mother, who later said, "I had always had a feeling that something was wrong, even when I watched Darryl on TV; he seemed so hostile, so angry. He was always getting into fights with other players. That was not the child I remember raising."

An explanation of drug addiction made sense—and created an emotional scene in Shapiro's office. Darryl wept and told Ruby he'd always been ashamed to tell her about the cocaine. But a similar confession didn't sway the Dodgers, who immediately placed Strawberry on the disabled list and got him into the Betty Ford Clinic. Strawberry nearly broke down in front of Claire, too, apologizing for the humiliation he had caused himself, his family, and the organization. The general manager said, "I genuinely felt bad for Darryl . . . I tried so many times to reach him, but I was never sure I could get through his wall. Of course, I had my suspicions drugs were involved, but we never had any real evidence."

Lasorda, however, wasn't so benevolent. "When people are late for meetings, and you don't show up for games, what kind of signs do you get from that? You don't have to be a rocket scientist to know something else is controlling his mind. There comes a time when one door will close on you, and if you're so concerned with the door that closes, you'll never find the one that's open. So we're looking for the open door."

Lasorda went on to say a few weeks later that Strawberry's drug addiction was not a sickness but a weakness. "I think that

anyone who knowingly, and by their own choice, puts a substance in their body that is against the law, and will destroy
their careers, is being weak," he said. "I loved Darryl, but I
couldn't understand what he was doing to himself. No one
makes you do those things, and if you know it's so harmful,
why would you?" That posture was met harshly by Eric Davis.

"I don't appreciate what Tommy said, not then and not
now," said Davis. "I understand his frustration, losing an inte-
gral part of the lineup the day before the season started, but
for anyone to say drugs isn't a sickness, something has to be
wrong with you. Especially from a man who admitted he had
a sickness with food. You can't say one addiction is a sickness
and the other is not. If you eat too much and weigh three hundred pounds and you admit you have a problem, isn't that saying you have a sickness?

"There has to be more to this than meets the eye. There was
so much rage there, but Tommy never had the same rage
against Steve Howe. I mean, Darryl isn't the first guy to ever
go into rehab, and he sure isn't going to be the last. So what is
it that Tommy has against Straw? We did everything he asked
of us, including sign autographs. Shoot, we signed more autographs for Tommy [to give to his celebrity friends] than we
did for the fans."

Surely, as Strawberry entered the prestigious rehab clinic,
he knew he'd be unemployed the moment he got out. But he
also knew he needed some form of help because the one true
passion in his life, baseball, was slowly drying up on him.
Strawberry didn't care about hitting fastballs anymore, about
wearing Dodger blue, or making it to the Hall of Fame, which
had always been one of his favorite boasts. "I started to look at
myself and say, 'What the fuck have I done with my life?' If I
didn't stop, my kids were going to grow up dysfunctional like

me because their father wasn't around to help raise them. I was so tired of it all. I really decided I needed a change."

It was at the Betty Ford Clinic that Strawberry learned about addiction, about cross-addiction, about the enablers around him who made it possible for Strawberry to keep drinking and drugging. "Basically, I learned about staying away from the atmosphere that led me to drink in the first place. I'm talking about bars and women," Strawberry said. "If I'd known that ten years ago with the Mets . . . man."

On May 25, Strawberry walked into the law offices of Latham & Watkins in downtown Los Angeles accompanied by Shapiro and Players Association representative Gene Orza. Across from those three sat Claire and Dodgers general counsel Sam Fernandez. The parting was cold, clean, and final. The Dodgers cut Strawberry a check for $4,857,143: the balance of his 1994 salary, $2,357,143, and half of the $5 million he was owed for 1995. Strawberry shook hands with Claire. They wished each other well, and the outfielder walked outside, into the daylight, asking the baseball gods for one last chance.

Inside the office, Claire was reminded of a similar liberation.

"I'll never forget going to Maury Wills's place in the Marina when we knew for sure he had a drug problem," Claire told Mike Downey of the *L.A. Times.* "Don Newcombe goes with me. Maury's denying, denying, denying. We go over there and bang on his door, and we tell him he's going to an Orange County treatment center if Don has to drag him there. All the while, he's telling us to get the hell away from him, leave him alone.

"He's ashamed. He doesn't want to be there. Remember, this is one of the most famous players in Dodgers history. Maury's so nervous, he doesn't even register under his own name. He checks into the clinic as Don Claire. Eventually, he gets better, thank God. And one morning, Maury finally gets up in front of everyone and says, 'You know, my name's not really Don.' And the people there, they smile at him and say, 'No kidding.'

"And now, all these years later, I'll be down in Vero Beach taking a jog around the grounds and I'll look up and see Maury Wills out on the golf course. And he gives a little wave, and I give a little wave, and we don't have to speak. We know, we just know. Maury saved his life."

6

TROUBLE IN TAMPA

IT WAS NOVEMBER 1986 and everywhere around the country, televisions were still hypnotized by that same, unforgettable image—a simple ground ball whispering through Bill Buckner's legs. No other moment so perfectly captured the World Series between the Mets and the Red Sox. No other has ever been needed. The tenth inning of game six, which ended with Mookie Wilson's ground ball down the first-base line, should have been the final out of the inning and kept the game tied 5–5. Instead, thanks to the kindness of some October god who kept the ball from taking a final, comfortable bounce into Buckner's glove, the Mets completed a three-run rally that gave them a 6–5 win.

The Mets may have pulled off a miracle in beating the Orioles in the 1969 World Series, but nothing in franchise history could match game six's final scene after Ray Knight crossed home plate with the winning run.

There was a mountain of flesh at the plate, one Met piled atop another screaming in disbelief, some of them weeping openly. A photo of the celebration made it to the back cover of the Mets' media guide the next year, a touching shot of Dykstra climbing atop Strawberry, who was about to fall onto Mookie, who was already on top of Hernandez, who was near the bottom of the pile near Gooden, Rick Aguilera, and Lee Mazzilli. Each one of them had the same look, the same body language, which carried the same message: The World is ours.

Although the final game was still to be played, the Red Sox never had a chance. The ghost of Mookie's ground ball was everywhere in Shea on October 27, and the Mets recovered from an early 3–0 deficit to crush the Sox 8–5, and walk away as world champs. The Mets' World Series ring was on the front of the '87 media guide.

The Mets spoke brazenly about their destiny and their dynasty. "We are a great team; everyone has to admit that now," Gary Carter said in the postgame celebration. But no one could have known that the franchise's erosion began the moment Jesse Orosco struck out Marty Barrett for the final out in game seven. Ray Knight left as a free agent, Kevin Mitchell was sent away, too. And although Dwight Gooden wasn't going anywhere, some wondered what had happened to him during the course of the '86 season and certainly during the World Series.

Gooden had posted fine numbers during the regular season: 17-6, with a 2.84 ERA. He struck out two hundred batters, the third straight year he'd fanned at least that many. Yet something was wrong: there were seven fewer wins than in 1985, sixty-eight fewer strikeouts. It was more than just faded numbers, too. Gooden's fastball was missing some of its last-second explosion, and hitters were learning to stay away from any pitch above the belt. In his first two seasons, that fastball would start somewhere around the upper thighs, right in the hitter's power zone. Only by the time he'd finished swinging, the ball had risen at least a foot. Physicists have long insisted that a pitched ball cannot rise, but Carter said, "They never caught one of Dwight's fastballs." But in 1986 not only had his heater lost its magic, even his curveball suffered bouts of uncharacteristic ineffectiveness. Although it still broke in a huge top-to-bottom arc—a twelve o'clock to six o'clock break, as scouts would say—Gooden bounced many in the dirt.

All this might have been a mere case of the law of averages playing catch-up with Gooden. No one could have been expected to dominate as he did in 1985. That year, at 24-4 with a 1.53 ERA, Gooden led the National League in wins, strikeouts (268), and ERA and lost only one game after May 25. He became the youngest player ever to win the Cy Young Award and, by 1986, the only pitcher since 1900 to have two hundred strikeouts in each of his first three seasons.

"Dwight was as unhittable as any pitcher in this era," said Carter. "I can't tell you how many hitters we started out 0-2 against. Boom, strike one, strike two, the rest was child's play. There were times that hitters, major-league hitters, were up there trying not to strike out. That's how much Dwight had dominated."

With 1985 as a measuring stick, what other path could Gooden follow except eventually to rejoin the human race? Even so, he was only twenty, with at least ten glorious years ahead of him. Yet, less than a year later, Gooden showed the subtlest signs of decay and, privately, the Met front office wondered if drugs were at work, or at least if there was some truth to the rumors of his drug activity. Despite his claims not to have succumbed in earnest until the winter of 1987, the Mets had been hearing whispers to the contrary. On December 27, 1985, Hillsborough County detectives pulled over Gooden's car in the Ybor City section of Tampa. According to police reports, among the items found in it were a holstered pistol, $4,000 in cash, and a bag of baking soda, which is commonly used to cut cocaine and also acts as an agent in freebasing.

Gooden might have been able to explain the gun and the cash—he did live in a rough section of Tampa, and as a prominent athlete, he was clearly a target. And carrying lots of cash was an important status symbol to him. But the baking soda clearly disturbed the Mets. One club official acknowledged, "We had our suspicions that Dwight may have been significantly involved in drug activity before nineteen eighty-seven, but we couldn't prove it for sure, and we couldn't force him to take a drug test. Unless he came to us for help, we were powerless to intervene."

The Mets' concerns peaked during the World Series, when Gooden was 0-2 and pitched ineffectively in both appearances against the Red Sox. In game two, Gooden allowed eight hits and was charged with six runs in five innings' work as the Mets lost 9–3. After allowing three runs in the third inning, Gooden gave up a solo home run to Dave Henderson in the fourth and another one to Dwight Evans in the fifth.

In game five, Gooden's performance was even more disappointing. He pitched four complete innings, faced three batters in the fifth without retiring any of them, and was charged with nine hits and four runs as the Mets lost 4–2, falling behind 3–2 in the series. Had it not been for the miracle beneath Buckner's glove, Gooden's 0-2 record and 8.00 ERA would have been more closely scrutinized at the end of the Series. But the Mets' front office prepared for the worst when Gooden failed to attend the ticker-tape parade on Wall Street on October 28.

Gooden blamed the all-night celebration the Mets had had after winning game seven. He said his mistake was trying to catch a quick nap before the festivities on Wall Street began. Gooden said, "I called Jay [Horwitz, the publicity director] to tell him exactly where I'd been." But that didn't mean the Mets believed him. After Gooden returned to Tampa for the off season, they continued to receive disturbing reports of his nighttime activities. Gooden had been listed on the Hillsborough County Sheriff's Office surveillance reports as having visited a well-known drug haven, the Manila Bar & Restaurant on East Seventh Avenue in Ybor City. The police report was made available to Commissioner Peter Ueberroth, whose office then passed the information along to the Mets.

The reports were, in fact, true, as Gooden finally yielded to drugs that winter, after being offered some by a second cousin in Tampa. His flirtation with cocaine was brief after both the '84 and '85 seasons, as he tried the drug just once or twice each winter. In both instances, Gooden was too scared to use regularly, but in the late fall of 1986 he fell once and for all.

Gooden was at a party in Tampa in November and recalled, "They had a room with coke, beer, marijuana, and stuff. A couple of guys, one of them was a cousin, I think, said, 'Try some.' Another guy said, 'I know you've done it before. You're in the big leagues.' I left the room and went out and had a few drinks. I wasn't drunk, but I was starting to feel good. Then someone said, 'Why don't you give it a try?' I wanted to say no, but I didn't. That's when I did it. It made me hyper, it made me speak out more at the party. And that's when it picked up in the off season. After that, it was off to the races."

Gooden says he began using cocaine about once a week during the winter, and his lifestyle changed enough so that he was regularly being tracked by the police. What Gooden may or may not have known during the Mets' World Series celebrations was that Tampa was inching closer to a race war. In the span of four months during baseball's off season, four black men were killed at the hands of white police officers.

On November 30, a sixteen-year-old runaway named Franklin Lewis was chased by police after witnesses said he fired a .38 caliber handgun into a crowd of people during a street party. Lewis was shot by officers during the pursuit, although no handgun was ever found.

On February 13, 1987, Melvin Hair was killed by police responding to a call of domestic violence. According to neighbors who called 911, Hair was attempting to kill his mother with a kitchen knife. Officers wrestled him to the ground and applied a "carotid restraint hold." Hair died shortly afterward, and police determined he never had a knife.

On March 21, Anthony Denard Perkins stole a purse from a Pizza Hut manager and fled across Interstate 275. The officer responding to the scene pursued Perkins and, having been told that he'd fired a shot at the Pizza Hut manager, shot and killed Perkins. Although a gun was later found on Perkins, it had never been fired.

On April 5, two officers struggled with a drifter who was collecting empty bottles and cans in a vacant lot. In a fierce fight, the officers subdued the man but not before he stopped breathing. He later died, apparently of a heart attack.

In the wake of these deaths, there were at least forty incidents of black youths pelting passing cars with rocks and bottles, a reaction that startled the city's elders. Tampa had enjoyed relative calm since 1967, when the last riot was touched off after the police shot a burglar. Community leaders praised the ease with which whites and blacks assimilated throughout the sixties and seventies. But in the eighties, Tampa exploded economically: construction was up 466 percent, gross sales grew by 186 percent, and the city's population swelled by 20 percent. But the skyscrapers still didn't hide the city's slums or its growing legion of unhappy, unattached youth. Indeed, while Tampa was enjoying a rebirth, school attendance fell by 1.2 percent.

Henry Carley, head of the local chapter of the NAACP, told reporters, "As the eighties crept up, I think the blacks in this town began to feel that the promises of America were eluding them. They felt they had been flimflammed. They realized it was a lot easier for a young black male to be admitted to prison than to college."

Of the four incidents in which black men were killed by white police officers, however, none attracted the attention that an altercation on December 13, 1986, did. Gooden, his nephew Gary Sheffield, currently a star with the Florida Marlins, his friend Vance Lovelace, and three other companions were returning home from a University of South Florida basketball game when the police stopped Gooden, allegedly for driving erratically. Earlier, Gooden had noticed unmarked police cars following them almost constantly; they were so easy to identify, big Fords, usually dark brown or black with blackwall tires. So he was in a testy mood before an officer even asked for his license and registration. Although Gooden had not used drugs that evening, he had "messed around" with cocaine two nights earlier.

"The cops were after me that winter. No matter where I went or what I did, there was always some cop watching, always nearby," Gooden said. "It makes you crazy, knowing you're always being followed . . . and for what? I wasn't doing anything wrong, especially not that night. We'd just been to a USF game, and then we'd gone to Chili's for something to eat. We're at a red light, I'm in my Mercedes, Gary is in his Corvette, one of the other guys has a 280ZX, the cop sees all these black guys and decides, 'What the hell, we'll see what we've got.' He was just looking for trouble from the get. The whole thing was a setup."

The officer waited until Gooden pulled away from the stoplight, then turned his overhead lights on. Gooden steered his car to the side of the road and waited. Doc was the only member of the traveling caravan who had been pulled over, but his colleagues pulled over, too. Before he even took a step in Gooden's direction, the cop told Gooden to keep both his hands outside the driver's side window. Although it was standard police procedure, Gooden was startled to see, in his rearview mirror, that the cop had a hand on his pistol as he neared. Gooden said, "He'd made up his mind that I was a criminal."

"Let me see your license and registration," the cop said.

"I'm tired of you harassing me. I'm sick of this bullshit," Gooden shouted back.

"Shut your fucking mouth. Get out of the fucking car."

At this point, Gooden estimated that at least ten police cruisers had arrived on the scene, "maybe as many as fifteen or sixteen. It seemed like every cop in Tampa was there," he said.

Gooden's colleagues, sensing trouble, got out of their cars to help, and that only heightened the level of tension. For his part, Gooden did nothing to defuse the situation, feeling as if he'd reached his breaking point with the police.

"You still haven't told me why you stopped me," Gooden said.

"You got a big fucking mouth, you know that?" the cop said.

"Why'd you stop me?" Gooden said, pressing his point.

It wasn't long before the cop snapped, and Gooden was the target of what he called "a wave of punches and blows." While other officers were punching him, the first cop grabbed Gooden's hands, apparently in an attempt to hand-cuff him. Gooden resisted and heard several officers shouting, "He's going for the gun, he's going for the gun." Gooden said he had no such intention, insisting, "I was only trying to de-fend myself because, basically, they were beating the shit out of me.

"There was nothing I could do except take it," Gooden said. "They were using fists, their feet, their knees, even their flash-lights. I never got hit so hard in my life, so many times. They wouldn't stop. I remember a female cop hit me as hard as she could with her flashlight. She smoked me, right across the face. I heard them screaming, 'Break his fucking arm, the motherfucker'll never pitch again.' They went for my right arm. They knew exactly what they were doing."

At that point, Gooden felt a massive pair of forearms squeezing his neck, cutting off his air supply. Everyone in the neighborhood knew about the choke hold. It was the cops' great equalizer, designed not only to disable an assailant and end the fight but to teach a lesson about power and control. Gooden realized that if he struggled any longer, "I was gonna die right on the spot." Even though Gooden's eyes were open, his vision began to go dark. Panicking, Gooden not only stopped resisting but pretended to pass out, too.

"I went totally limp. I wanted them to think I was either unconscious or dead," Gooden later said. "That was the only thing that was going to save me from those guys." The forearms kept squeezing, though, and, for a half second, Gooden feared he was about to be murdered. But he heard a cop shout, "Let him go, he's out, he's out." Still pretending to be unconscious, Gooden felt himself being thrown in the back of one of the cruisers, safe, he thought, and on his way to a hospital. He would explain the incident to his agent, Jim Neader, the next morning and no doubt to the press and to the Mets. "What, exactly, did I do so wrong?" Gooden kept asking himself as the cruiser wound through the streets of Tampa, strangely absent of its lights or sirens.

Gooden wanted to look up and see where they were going so silently, but he knew better than to make another sound. In a few minutes, the police car stopped and a policeman turned to him and said, "Get out." Gooden got to his feet and "realized we were near the railroad tracks."

There was no one around. Was he about to be murdered? "I wasn't sure, to be honest," he said. Actually, quite the opposite was about to take place. Tampa police knew exactly how it would look if the city's most famous athlete showed up in public so badly beaten. So they called for a paramedic to dress Gooden's wounds before they took him to a hospital. When he was ready to face doctors, the cops made sure a black cop was placed in the cruiser with him.

The most significant event of the night still hadn't taken place, though. At the hospital, Gooden was forced to submit to a drug test. Despite the fact that he'd used coke only forty-eight hours earlier, the test results were negative. That's when Gooden came to believe his metabolism was too quick for any drug test, feeling that despite his stepped-up drug use that winter, he could safely tell the Mets he would submit to drug tests in spring training.

Of course, the incident with the police was reported throughout the country, and Gooden's name was further soiled. Chris Hoyer—chief assistant to State Attorney Bill James and the man who prosecuted Gooden—told *Sports Illustrated* that Gooden's involvement in the fistfight and his headlong plunge into Tampa's drug scene "did not come as a surprise . . . I know a lot of people in the law enforcement community who have been concerned about [his] welfare for a couple of years."

Gooden and four members of his traveling party that night were arrested and charged with battery of a police officer and violently resisting arrest. Although he felt he had grounds for brutality charges against police, Gooden pleaded no contest and was sentenced to three years' probation and 160 hours of community service. Gooden let the matter drop because, he said, "I wanted to put it behind me. It wasn't worth it. It was better to just move on." Gary Sheffield, Lovelace, and another friend also pleaded no contest and were given two years' probation. The fifth party was absolved because he was a juvenile.

It was a dark moment in Gooden's life, not easily forgotten. Mets general manager Frank Cashen met with Gooden after the incident and asked him, "What's the problem? Is there anything you want to talk about?" Cashen did not mention drugs, nor did Gooden volunteer any information. Instead, he retreated from the press, knowing his side of the story would never be accepted. Gooden continued to be followed by police, almost to the time he and family moved to St. Petersburg later that winter. "I didn't feel like every single cop was out to get me, but after a while you start to get paranoid," he said. Gooden's friends harbored more than just anger. Some wanted revenge. They talked about getting even with the cops, about the way they had continued hurting Gooden long after he had been subdued and about the general arrogance they had displayed toward Tampa's inner-city blacks. Gooden's solution was to move across the bay to St. Petersburg, a quieter and gentler community. But Gooden's friends had a different plan.

He learned about it a week later one night in the front seat of a friend's car. The friend's name, Gooden has said, will never be revealed. Nor will the identities of the two others, in the backseat. "They were close to me, that's all I'm going to say," Gooden said. Close enough that they were willing to take on any cop that attempted to harass them that night. They had come to pick Gooden up at his house, and, as he got in the car, he noticed a .38 caliber pistol on the floor next to the driver's feet.

"What's that for?" Gooden asked, already knowing the answer.

"We're gonna fuck up the first cop who fucks with us," the friend said.

"Yeah, a little surprise," a voice from the back said. "Motherfuckers."

Gooden understood about revenge, about how unfair the cops had been—not just to him but to any black citizen who needed the benefit of the doubt. Like Strawberry, Gooden had never played the race card in his life, never once felt uncomfortable in a Met clubhouse full of white faces. But this time he was angry. He was not entirely self-destructive, however.

Gooden knew the night could only end up one way—badly for him and his friends. Someone was going to get hurt, maybe worse than that, and, either way, Gooden knew his career would end. He couldn't let it go, not like this.

Doc thought of his parents, of how much his baseball career meant to them. He thought of his father, especially, how proud he'd been the day his son became a Met and extended the family tree farther than he had. Dwight had bought his father a satellite dish just so he could watch every game his son was pitching. Gooden thought of the Mets themselves. Only two months earlier, they had told themselves the good times would never end. Gooden remembered the way he and Strawberry had felt, their faces dripping with champagne. What would the Mets say now if they knew their teammate was in a car with three guys intent on firing that pistol into a police officer's face?

The car had traveled no more than half a block. Once it reached the first stop sign, Gooden knew there was no turning back. He was at a crossroads, just as he had been five years earlier with Hawk, the drug dealer. That time he failed. This time the stakes were too steep for a similar mistake.

"Stop the car," he said quietly.

The driver looked at him, eyes slightly widened in disbelief.

"You heard me. Stop," Gooden said. "I'm getting out."

He opened the door and got out. None of them ever said a word to Gooden. They waited a moment or two to see if he was kidding. Instead, he looked in and said, "I can't do it." After a few seconds, they drove off. Gooden went home, and that night he prayed. Gooden wasn't much into religion, not like his Baptist mother, but he sensed someone was going to die that night. It was either his friends or whatever cop who would have been unlucky enough to stop them.

When Gooden woke up the next morning, he was scared to call his friends, afraid no one would answer. He immediately turned on the radio to hear if there had been any trouble in Tampa the night before. He heard nothing. Somehow, the plan for revenge failed to materialize, although Gooden never found out why. He never asked, and the incident was never mentioned again.

7

A CRY FOR HELP

THERE ARE TWO versions as to why Dwight Gooden agreed to be tested for drugs in the off season following the 1986 World Series, even though he was already involved with cocaine. There is the Mets' account, which says that Gooden and his agent, Jim Neader, volunteered for the tests and, in fact, insisted on them.

According to Joe McIlvaine and Al Harazin, who were Met vice presidents at the time, Gooden first raised the issue less than a month after the Series. The club said that in Gooden's words they could test, "every week, every two days, as often as anyone wanted, and it can be forever."

Neader formally brought the matter to the Mets' attention in December and repeated the intention two months later while negotiating Gooden's contract. Harazin told reporters he found Gooden's and Neader's repeated requests "kind of overreacting. I thought it was a little unusual."

Around March 22, Harazin and Neader agreed that Gooden would be tested once during spring training and as soon as possible. Gooden, however, would have the option to postpone the test. Furthermore, the Mets were given permission to test two other times during the regular season. On March 24, Harazin and Neader met again, and the agent readily agreed that Gooden should be tested for "everything."

Harazin asked Neader, "What if for some reason he tests positive, then what? If that happens, we're in a very difficult position. We'd have to inform the commissioner." Harazin asked only because the rumors had been so persistent, that there was no ignoring them. Neader asked for twenty-four hours before answering but, after conferring with Gooden, told Harazin the next day, "Go ahead, test for everything."

Today, Gooden agrees he gave the Mets full permission to test him—but only because they had come to him first. "Someone on the team turned me in," Gooden said. "Steve Garland came to me and said, 'The front office has been hearing rumors about you.' I'm not sure who it was that was talking about me, not even today, but I have my ideas. Someone gave me up to protect themselves."

"That was the rumor, that someone squealed on Doc," Gary Carter agreed. "I would have to say it was someone on the team that was already into drugs himself."

The suspects stretched across half the roster by Gooden's and Strawberry's count. If it could be any of a dozen Mets, the question was: why would even one of them have a grudge against Gooden? He was universally liked in the clubhouse and held in even higher regard by some. "We loved Dwight as much as we could possibly love a teammate," Bob Ojeda said flatly. "You never, ever heard anyone say a bad word about the guy, not to his face or behind his back. And remember, that was a tough clubhouse. A lot of shit went on in there, both on and off the record."

The only motives for another Met to betray him, Gooden reasoned, were either revenge or self-protection. Gooden obviously had no quarrel with the team's most influential players, captains Carter and Hernandez. He certainly was tight with Strawberry. None of the other pitchers seemed angry with him. Revenge seemed unlikely, but what about self-preservation? Here the choices became fuzzier.

Strawberry's name had been linked with drugs for more than a year in New York. Could the Mets have confronted him and been led to Gooden? Would Darryl do such a thing? Doc shook his head in disbelief. There was another far-fetched possibility, too, and its roots reached back to the charter flight back from Houston on October 15, 1986, after game six of the National League Championship Series against the Astros.

The Mets, who were down 3–0 going into the ninth inning, were facing a near certain defeat, and with the virtually unbeatable Mike Scott waiting for them in game seven, it seemed as if the season was over. But Lenny Dykstra led off with a pinch-hit triple, sparking a three-run rally that sent the Mets into a sixteen-inning sojourn. They finally went ahead for good, 7–6, on Strawberry's bloop double and Ray Knight's RBI single. The game ended when Jesse Orosco struck out Kevin Bass in the bottom of the sixteenth with the tying and winning runs on base. The game lasted 4:42 and was so riveting sportswriter Maury Allen of the *New York Post* said, "I'm completely exhausted, and I haven't written a word yet."

The Mets were delirious in their celebration, both in the clubhouse after the game and on the plane ride home to New York. There was nonstop drinking, and a food fight at thirty thousand feet that resulted in $10,000 worth of damage to the

TWA 727. It has become Met legend by now that Frank Cashen presented Davey Johnson with a letter from the airline demanding repayment. In full view of his players, Johnson tore up the letter and told Cashen, "Let [owners] Doubleday and Wilpon pay. If it wasn't for us, there wouldn't have been a World Series."

But during the flight there was a disturbing incident. According to Gooden and several other players, the lavatory door accidentally opened and inside the Mets saw one of their teammates with his face buried in a mound of cocaine. "We all saw it, and we decided, 'Nope, we didn't see anything,'" Gooden said. The player quickly closed the door, and nothing else was ever said. No Met has ever publicly identified the player, but following the World Series the rumors swirled around Wally Backman, the tough little second baseman who smoked cigarettes as furiously as Keith Hernandez and played ball with the same fearlessness. Backman and Dykstra were so vital to the Mets as their number one and two hitters that Mike Schmidt once said, "Those guys are the real MVPs of the team." Backman had played parts of three seasons with the Mets in the early eighties but it seemed as though his career as a major leaguer was over when they demoted him to Triple-A in 1983.

Fortunately for Backman, he found an up-and-coming manager at Tidewater named Davey Johnson, who liked his second baseman's spirit. Backman responded to his manager, hitting .316, and in 1984, when Johnson was asked to save the Mets, he brought Backman with him. The marriage seemed as if it would last forever, or at least as long as the Mets' golden era. But there were rumors about Backman that were fueled by the flight from Houston to New York.

To this day, he denies ever having used cocaine on the airplane. "I would have to have been a complete idiot to do something like that," Backman said. "I've been hearing the same rumors about that plane from the day of the flight, and I've been hearing it for ten years ever since. Sometimes I think that's all the Mets remember me for."

Backman was so disturbed by the damage to his reputation that he confronted Frank Cashen during the World Series. He said, "Frank, whatever you heard about me on the plane, it isn't true." According to Backman, the general manager responded, "Wally, I have no idea what you're talking about." Nevertheless, after the Series Backman agreed to fly back to New York from his home in Oregon to meet with psychiatrist Dr. Allan Lans.

"I went back to New York on my own, walked into Smithers, and told Dr. Lans, 'It's a bogus rumor,'" Backman said. Whether the Mets believed him remains questionable. Backman was traded two years later, and although he claimed to have asked to be let go, not wanting to be a sideline witness to Gregg Jefferies's coronation as the infield savior, he also conceded, "I never got away from the rumor altogether. The Mets might've thought I had a drug problem. It probably had an effect on them trading me."

Some Mets wonder if Backman may have inadvertently implicated Gooden in his attempt to clear his own name, although the second baseman insisted, "I was always very, very close to Dwight. I considered him a friend. I know this, though: the day he tested positive was a pretty bad one for all of us."

Gooden isn't sure to this day who the culprit is, although he says, "I have a few theories. It was someone trying to take the heat off himself. But I can't be sure. Until I ever get positive proof, it's better not to point the finger. Still, that person knows who it is."

The fateful day was Thursday, March 26, when Steve Garland took a urine sample from Gooden and sent it to St. Petersburg General Hospital. Gooden admitted he was caught off guard by the Mets' haste in testing him. "When I said it was okay to test, I had no idea it was going to be the very next day."

Still, he decided not to postpone the test because, he recalled, "I didn't want anyone to have any suspicions. It would've looked bad, calling it off." And Gooden was also confident the test results would be negative, despite the fact that he'd used cocaine two days earlier. Gooden believed this, remembering that he'd beaten the drug test after his arrest in December, despite having used cocaine forty-eight hours earlier.

"The point is, you never think you're gonna get caught," Gooden said.

But on Monday, March 30, Cashen and Harazin received the result, which revealed there was cocaine in Gooden's system. The Mets waited two days—an incubation period Cashen would call "the most agonizing forty-eight hours of my life"—before informing their star pitcher, because they first had to contact Commissioner Ueberroth and then the club's board of directors. The choice Gooden faced was not pleasant: he had to either enter into a drug rehabilitation program or else be suspended without pay for one year.

The task that confronted the Mets' executives wasn't easy, either. On Tuesday, March 31, Harazin warned publicity director Jay Horwitz, "Tomorrow is going to be one of the worst days of your professional career. Don't ask me to explain. I can't. But just be ready when Frank asks for your help."

On Wednesday, April 1, as he pulled into the parking lot of the Mets' spring-training facility, Gooden was intercepted by vice president Joe McIlvaine, who said Cashen wanted to see him immediately. Gooden was so unaware of the impending crisis, he said, "I thought they wanted to add some years to my contract." Instead, the general manager told Gooden the test results had shown traces of cocaine in his system.

"This is a joke, right? This is an April Fool's thing, right, Frank?" Gooden remembered asking.

Cashen stood silently in front of his pitcher, wondering how to make him understand.

"No, Dwight, I'm very serious about this. You need to make a phone call right now. Is there someone you can reach out to?"

One last time, Gooden hid behind a wall of denial, claiming the test must have been a mistake, that he didn't use cocaine and never had. But finally he broke down and cried. And even more distressing to the employers of baseball's most dominant pitcher, Dwight Gooden didn't know whom to call.

"He just sat there, befuddled," McIlvaine said. "Here's a guy who's been on top of the world, and at a moment when he most needed help, he didn't know who he would ask."

Gooden wanted desperately to reach out to his parents, but he knew the heartbreak that would follow his announcement. In fact, Doc knew the pain would be so keen in the Gooden household that he continued to think of ways to spare his parents, even to the point of lying about the test results. He left the Mets' complex a few minutes after being told of his options: rehab or a season-long suspension without pay. Even though Doc didn't consider himself an addict, there were economic factors involved in his decision. "My parents were retired and my father was ill and on kidney dialysis. I had to keep playing. I couldn't afford to sit out a year."

For the first time that he could remember, Gooden was making the reverse commute on the Frankland Bridge, never having noticed before how bad the traffic was going into

Tampa at 8 A.M. So this is what it feels like to be on the outside, Gooden thought. Real people going to real jobs. And none of them had any idea the game's most famous pitcher was sitting in the same traffic jam.

"The drive took forever," he recalled. "The whole time, I'm thinking, What do I say? How do I say it? I mean, how do you explain a thing like that to your parents? I'm sure my mom had some idea something was going on in my life that previous winter because I'd be out so late, and sometimes I wouldn't even come home at all. But whenever she asked me if there was something wrong, I would just deny it."

When Gooden finally pulled into the driveway of his parents' house, he decided to tell the truth as bluntly as possible: "I walked into the living room with my parents there and said, 'I've got some bad news, and I've got some good news. The bad news is that I tested positive for cocaine. They found it in my system. The good news is that I'm getting help for it.'" Gooden's parents went silent, as if the words made no sense. The tears flowed almost immediately afterward, but Gooden's mother recovered far quicker than Doc ever imagined she would. She seemed glad that her son was getting help and that he had taken such a bold step forward.

The Mets themselves, including Strawberry, reacted with all the proper shock, although most of them were no doubt relieved to see Gooden, and not them, being disciplined. Strawberry said at the time, "It could have happened to me. I just had the right people around me to advise me growing up. You have to surround yourself with people who really care about you." Strawberry went as far as to call Gooden's boyhood friends from Tampa "leeches" and urged Doc to leave Florida altogether.

"Even if you hear rumors, sometimes you don't want to believe them," Wally Backman added. "Maybe that's what it was. Look at the guy. He's the best pitcher in baseball over the last three years. Probably eighty percent of the rumors aren't true. It was just as easy to think something like that was in the eighty percent category."

Inside the Mets' facility, the press was kept outside the clubhouse while the team was officially notified. Davey Johnson took the news the hardest. Sitting at his desk in his office, he said, "I just heard the news, and I still can't believe it. I really am shocked. Totally shocked."

"A couple of times during the nineteen eighty-six season, I asked Dwight, 'Is everything okay?' But I never asked him point-blank about drugs," Gary Carter said. "It never occurred to me that Dwight was having a problem like that. And even if I did, how do you go ask someone if he's on drugs?"

Certainly, there were still suspicions about other Mets, specifically Strawberry. Former Met George Foster, who had been released in August 1986 after questioning whether the Mets made personnel decisions on the basis of race, said that besides Gooden at least "two other" Mets were using cocaine.

The Mets, who parted with Foster on bitter terms, were predictably harsh when they learned about his accusation. "If he saw anything, then why didn't he tell me?" Davey Johnson said. "He never said a word."

"Foster never worried about us before that," Backman added. "Why was he worrying about the team all of a sudden?"

"I'm not surprised he said that," Keith Hernandez said cryptically.

Foster was right, of course, at least about Strawberry. But if Darryl wasn't safe from drugs, he was at least beyond the reach of drug testing. For the moment the Mets had their hands full with Gooden, who was about to spend twenty-eight days at the Smithers Alcoholism and Treatment Center.

At 11:15 A.M., April 3, 1987, Gooden entered the forty-three-bed facility that had been opened in 1973 thanks to a $5 million grant from R. Brinkley Smithers. Although it was a new world for Gooden, the Mets had successfully treated one of their own before, relief pitcher Neil Allen, who in 1983 sought help for alcohol addiction.

Gooden arrived at Smithers in a gray van that had picked him up at La Guardia Airport, right off the tarmac. There would be no exposure to the public, and as he walked through the front doors of the center, a crush of reporters would only see Doc with head bowed, refusing to answer any questions. That was the last anyone would see of Gooden as he entered a miniature hell where he often cried himself to sleep, surrounded by what he called "real, hard-core junkies." In Gooden's mind, he was just a recreational user who merely suffered the misfortune of failing a drug test. He was not an addict, not by his own standards. He did not belong there.

Gooden was assigned a single bed, a nightstand, and a lamp and shared his dormitory-like room with three other patients. His day would begin at 7 A.M., and, like every other patient, Gooden was given chores before he participated in mandatory lectures, group therapy sessions, and one-on-one meetings with counselors. He was also given reading and writing assignments that forced him to explore, both for his counselors' benefit and his own, the roots of his involvement with drugs.

Although there was time allotted each day for exercise, Gooden did little more than climb the facility's stairs. The food was poor. With a diminished appetite and limited opportunities for physical fitness, Gooden left Smithers ten pounds lighter and considerably softer. Needless to say, he didn't pick up a ball in those twenty-eight days, either. But Gooden also walked out the door with the belief that he was an addict but that his addiction was not to the extent of other patients.

He had listened to the stories and was horrified in particular by one addict who said the only needle-free spot on his body was his neck, into which he also shot heroin. Other addicts talked about the bingeing that came with coke and crack, how it could consume entire blocks of days before one realized he hadn't eaten or bathed. In comparison, Gooden's own accounts seemed mild, as he described how he would use cocaine at parties with girls in Tampa and only once a week at that.

"They said, 'C'mon, man, you're lying.' " Gooden recalled. "They didn't believe me. I realized that I didn't belong in that place."

Gooden was still in denial as he walked out of Smithers, a fact he readily acknowledges a decade later. Had he accepted that he was a recovering addict, and would be for the rest of his life, it's possible he would have had fewer brushes with cocaine in the nineties. But the public humiliation was too great for someone so young, so talented. After all, nothing—and no one—had been able to defeat Gooden to this point. He wasn't about to bow down to cocaine.

He was ready to conquer the world on June 5, the day of his comeback, although for the first time, he didn't know an entirely supportive public. It was Dick Young of the *New York Post* who wrote a column headlined STAND UP AND BOO on the night Gooden returned. It was Young's belief that fans should boo Gooden for his involvement with drugs but then cheer him for fighting back. The negative half of Young's message was never heard, though. Young was unquestionably the country's most influential sports columnist through the sixties and seventies, but on this day, his words evaporated before the masses. Met fans cheered Gooden wildly as he easily defeated the Pirates, 5–1.

Still, the *Post*'s headline was so inflammatory, so unforgiving, that Gooden vowed never to forget the wound. He and Young never spoke to each other again, and when the columnist died on August 31 of that same year, Gooden—as well as Keith Hernandez—refused to honor the columnist's legacy. "I've got nothing to say about the man," Gooden said. "Let's let it go at that."

Finally, at the end of June 1987, Gooden told his side of the story. In retrospect, it was a warning sign that more trouble awaited. Both the *New York Post* and *Newsday* ran a lengthy interview with Gooden, in which he bristled at the suggestion that he was an addict.

"I am not a junkie, I never was," Gooden said. "I made a mistake messing around with [cocaine] the first time, and it's something I never should've done. I can't blame anyone but myself . . . it's embarrassing and sad, especially because of all the people who look up to you. When I did [cocaine] it was fine. But after I did it, I'd wake up the next day, after the high had left, and say, 'What am I doing? What if the police catch me? What if my family finds out?' At the time you're doing it, you don't ask those questions. It's not like someone forced me to do it. I guess I could've ended up like Len Bias."

Gooden insisted he had no further urges to use the drug, that he never pitched high in '86 or any other year, and that he never brought cocaine into the clubhouse. But the confession wasn't entirely honest, because Gooden said, "No one else [among the Mets] was using it, and I don't think anybody's doing it now. I could tell if they were, especially now that I can read the signs."

IT WAS SEVEN years before Gooden tested positive again. To outsiders, he had beaten the drug; indeed, as the seasons passed, memories of Gooden's crisis seemed to fade, replaced more by his on-field troubles than anything else. No matter how hard he tried, Gooden was unable to re-create the magic his fastball had possessed in 1985. Despite missing two months of the '87 season, Gooden went on to win fifteen games, a very respectable total, but his ERA climbed over 3.00 for the first time in his career.

In 1988, Gooden was a solid 18-9 with a 3.19 ERA, and the Mets captured the National League East with a one-hundred-win season. But there was a strange negative karma about the Mets, even after they won thirty-one of their first forty-four games. The team lost its energy in June and July and, in one stretch of thirty-nine innings on the West Coast, scored just three runs. Frank Cashen said, "In all my years in baseball, I've never seen a club with this much talent play so poorly for so long." Hernandez went even further, calling the '88 Mets "a bunch of Little Leaguers."

Only Gregg Jefferies's arrival in September resurrected the Mets, as he hit .321 after being called up. Yet October crushed the Mets, as the Dodgers beat them in a seven-game National League Championship Series. The turning point was a two-run homer that Gooden allowed Mike Scioscia in the ninth inning of game four, with the Mets leading the series two games to one. Gooden was only three outs shy of a 4–2 win, which would have left the Mets just one game away from the World Series—and Doc's first-ever postseason victory. But Scioscia's blast into the Mets' bullpen in right field tied the game at 4–4 and led to the Dodgers' eventual 5–4 win in twelve innings.

In 1989, Doc suffered his first serious injury, a muscle tear in the back of the shoulder that limited him to 118 innings. In 1990, he rebounded to a strong 19-7 season, and even though his ERA swelled to a career-high 3.83, he struck out an impressive 223 batters in 232 innings, his best ratio since 1985. But as the years blurred one into the next, the Mets were in full decline. In fact, with Hernandez and Carter already gone, 1990 was the last summer that meant much at Shea. By 1991, Strawberry, Gooden, and Davey Johnson had used up all the charms that had protected them throughout the eighties.

Strawberry was in L.A., slowly being pulled down by his childhood demons. Davey was out of a job forty-two games into the season, embarking on a three-year blacklist, the price tag for all those years when he drank too much and argued too loudly with Frank Cashen. And Gooden? He found out how mortal his arm really was on September 7, 1991, the day he underwent arthroscopic surgery to repair a torn labrum in the right shoulder and a partial tear in the rotator cuff. That was the last winning season Gooden had.

Through it all, though, he never gave the Mets reason to doubt his commitment to remain drug-free. Through at least the 1990 season, Gooden was subjected to the tests, three times every week. Officials from the commissioner's office would arrive at Shea, unannounced, and ask Gooden for a urine sample. And without fail, he took the tests and passed. Steve Garland said, "They would take it about three times a week, and not always on the same three days. There'd be a call in the morning, telling me to make the arrangements with Dwight. And then in the afternoon they'd be there. With that little notice, there was no way he could've been cheating."

Just to be sure, Gooden would be directly observed while producing the urine sample, unlike New York Giants star Lawrence Taylor, who claimed to have beaten drug tests by asking teammates to produce the samples for him. No, Gooden

Dwight, age eleven, with his parents, Dan and Ella Mae, providers of a comfortable and easy childhood.

Gooden, December 1986, answering questions about a brawl with Tampa police. With him is attorney Ron Cacciatore.

Darryl Strawberry, with daughter Diamond Nicole—a bright spot in the otherwise turbulent 1980s.

Gooden and Strawberry with Mike Tyson: three up-and-coming stars who would soon discover the hard side of stardom.

Gooden, April 1987, leaving Smithers Alcoholism and Treatment Center in Manhattan after a twenty-eight-day stay for drug abuse. It would be seven years before Gooden would test positive again.

Strawberry, March 1990, leaving a hearing regarding his arrest two months earlier for threatening his wife with a handgun. With Strawberry is Mets psychiatrist Dr. Allan Lans.

The late Bill Goodstein, Strawberry's attorney, spring training, 1992. Despite his fiery temper, Strawberry said of Goodstein, "the man saved my career."

Strawberry and Gooden, opponents in 1991, joined by, from left, Mets reliever John Franco and Dodgers manager Tommy Lasorda. Happy faces . . . but not for long.

Strawberry, July 1990, with nickname "Straw" shaved into his head. Within three months, he would be on his way to Los Angeles.

Strawberry with his second wife, Charisse, after sentencing in White Plains, N.Y., for tax evasion in April 1995. Spared jail time, Darryl called it "a blessed day for me."

Gooden, June 1994, after a forty-seven-day stint on the disabled list with a broken toe.

Gooden, with, from left, agent Ray Negron and twelve-step counselor Ron Dock, August 1995.

Strawberry, June 1995, playing for the Gulf Coast Yankees before joining the big-league team in the Bronx. The big, looping home-run swing remained intact after so many years.

was drug-free between 1987 and 1994—and with Strawberry gone, Kevin Mitchell traded, and Hernandez, Backman, Dykstra, and all the other inner-circle Mets weeded out, the front office was sure it had routed its drink-and-drug lifestyle.

But that wasn't entirely true. While Gooden was indeed cocaine-free, he continued to drink. In fact, he resumed drinking as soon as he left Smithers, and he never stopped. In 1986, when Gooden first began drinking heavily, he would abstain only on the two nights prior to taking the mound, and that pattern resumed in 1987. Why? Gooden explained, "It was a way of proving to myself, and everyone else, that I wasn't an addict. It was like I was saying, 'Look, I'm tough enough to drink and not go any further.'"

Perhaps it was a form of rebellion against the smothering to which Gooden was subjected. It started in 1984, when he was immediately hailed as the greatest prodigy the game had ever known. The Mets knew that Gooden was more fragile than Strawberry and made sure never to let the out-of-town media and magazine journalists get too close.

Interview requests were handled through the public relations office, and even though the Mets meant well, the result was that much of Gooden's persona became a lie. Even after Gooden had checked in and out of Smithers—logically a time period in which he would have done the most growing and soul-searching—the Mets continued to keep him closely monitored. On the day of his first public workout at Shea, reporters were forced to wait in the auxiliary pressroom, which had a guard posted at the door. The media was even denied access to the press box. For weeks after Gooden returned to the Mets' starting rotation, he was instructed to answer questions only about baseball. Anyone who attempted to probe into Gooden's drug history was immediately cut off by a member of the P.R. staff.

Finally, when Gooden did open up to *Newsday* and the *Post* in late June, he did so on his own, without the club's prior knowledge or permission, and was harshly reprimanded by the front office. The two reporters who broke the story were shunned for weeks by P.R. director Horwitz.

The problem with Gooden's drinking was that it acted as a gateway to cocaine. He admitted as much in 1987, when he said, "You could put a bag of cocaine in front of me right now, and I would have no desire to use it. But if I'm drunk, then it's a different story."

As Strawberry discovered a few years earlier, the pressure to drink among the Mets was great, especially on charter flights. Not that Gooden would ever dare dream of acting on his cocaine urges on a team plane or in front of teammates. That much he kept separate. In fact, not one Met ever claimed to have seen Gooden do drugs, not even Strawberry, who said, "Doc and I never partied together."

But Gooden was certainly part of the team's alcohol culture, and he was seen in bars on road trips. "It's like I wanted to prove that I was still one of them. I wanted to be seen," Gooden said. Every city had its favorite spots. The Chez Paris in Montreal, AJ's in St. Louis, all of Rush Street in Chicago, The Clark Bar in Pittsburgh, The Red Onion in San Diego. These places were important to the Mets, so much so that Dave Magadan said, "It got to the point where some of the players thought of road trips in terms of which bars they'd be able to hit. The drinking and nightlife became at least as important, if not more so, than the baseball."

For Gooden, the drinking kept the spark of drug addiction alive. What puzzled him, in retrospect, is that he drank with the full knowledge of Dr. Allan Lans, the psychiatrist who oversaw his aftercare program. Unlike Keith Hernandez,

Gooden would never touch a beer at the ballpark. But among his alcohol-related activities was occasionally having dinner with Dr. Lans, and at these times, Gooden would drink.

"Dr. Lans was my friend, and I would never point a finger and say it was someone else's fault. But why did Dr. Lans let me keep drinking all those years?" Gooden asked. "We had a professional relationship at first, and then we grew closer. We'd go out to dinner, and right in front of him, I'd order wine or beer. Don't get me wrong, it's not like I had their permission: no one ever said, 'As long as you're drinking and not drugging, it's okay.' But I was still the patient. I was still sick."

Reached for comment at the Kirby Forensic Psychiatric Center in Manhattan where he now works, Dr. Lans said, "I don't want to comment about that. I'd really rather not have anything to do with those two guys."

No one ever doubted Lans's good intentions or his professional skill. But by 1989 he had severed his ties with Smithers and confined his practice to working with the Mets, unwittingly throwing himself into clubhouse politics. In September of 1989, Lans came under fire for calling the team meeting that erupted into a near fistfight between Strawberry and Davey Johnson. The incident took place only days after Strawberry and Kevin McReynolds were found in the clubhouse at Chicago's Wrigley Field undressing when the Mets, behind in the game, were still batting in the ninth inning.

When the Mets rallied, Strawberry was forced to rush back to the field, literally pulling his pants up as he ran from the clubhouse to the dugout. Both players were fined by Johnson, and when the tension lingered into the next day, it was Lans who called for the summit.

Gooden did have a special relationship with Lans; Lans was the doctor in charge of Gooden's life after Smithers. But other players weren't as open to a psychiatrist's presence in the clubhouse. Tim Teufel said, "I didn't think we needed a psychiatrist to win ball games." And, more harshly, Randy Myers said, "He plays cards with guys like he's trying to be one of their buddies. It's like a fan who's hanging out in the clubhouse. It's one thing to have someone available if a player wants someone to talk to. It's another thing to have him hanging around every day."

Lans, no doubt, had to expect some criticism when he accepted a full-time position with the Mets. After all, not every athlete wants or needs a counselor, and even though he was a Met employee, Lans was still walking into hostile territory. Any reporter will tell you a clubhouse is a player's sanctuary. You are a guest and never allowed to forget that.

But one Met executive asked, "What was Allan supposed to do, slap the drink out of his hand? Dwight was given the tools to work with at Smithers, but if he refused to listen to the message, whose fault is that? At some point, you take responsibility for your own recovery."

It was in 1992 that Gooden believed his drinking had grown "pretty much out of control." It was his way of dealing with cocaine urges. Unlike previous years, when alcohol had led him to reach for the drug, now he was simply reaching for another drink. "I was drinking more and drinking more often," he said, "graduating from beer to vodka."

There were reasons behind Gooden's accelerated drinking. His father had suffered a broken hip in a fall at home, and the surgery was complicated, indeed, life-threatening, given his kidney condition. Surgery on Gooden's rotator cuff was also the most tangible sign that not only were his days of dominating hitters over but, sooner or later, his career would end, too. And then there were the Mets themselves, who, four short years after their one-hundred-win season in 1988, became the worst team in baseball.

How did it come apart so fast? The clubhouse was missing its most energetic characters, the ones who had made the Mets so alive, so arrogant, and, ultimately, so unbeatable. One by one, Gooden's friends disappeared. The last link with the past came in September of '92, when the Mets traded David Cone to the Blue Jays. In return the Mets received two very iffy prospects, Ryan Thompson and Jeff Kent, and the emotional void Cone's departure created was huge.

Gooden said, "It felt like there was nobody left on the team I could really talk to." Oh, there was Bobby Bonilla and Eddie Murray and Vince Coleman. Those were Al Harazin's contributions to Shea now that he'd inherited the general manager's title. But Gooden seemed to disappear after games, at least from the sight of his teammates. Instead, he returned to his roots of 1984, when his social world was built around P.R. man Jay Horwitz, equipment manager Charlie Samuels, and Vinnie Greco, Samuels's assistant. Perhaps Gooden retreated because he wasn't pitching well and the team was performing even more appallingly.

In 1992, Gooden finished under .500 for the first time in his career, posting a 10-13 won-lost record. He failed to throw a single shutout. His ERA was 3.67, second highest of his nine years. Part of the problem was the play of the Mets themselves. Despite a $44 million payroll, a new manager in Jeff Torborg, a new general manager in Harazin, and plenty of new faces, the Mets lost ninety games, finishing next to last, twenty-four games behind the Pirates. They finished last in the majors with a .235 batting average and set a major-league record for hitting just seventeen triples. In short, the '92 Mets couldn't hit and couldn't run, and their ace, Dwight Gooden, couldn't help them.

The next year was almost a clone of 1992, as Gooden and the Mets continued to unfold. While the club finished dead last in the East with 103 losses—which cost Torborg and Harazin their jobs—Gooden suffered his second straight sub-.500 season, going 12-15. In 1994, Gooden was again struggling, going 3-4 and on injury-rehab after suffering a broken toe. Gooden said, "I was more depressed than I'd ever been in my career. Things weren't going right anymore, nothing was."

Charlie Samuels said Gooden's depression went deeper than anyone knew. "He came into the clubhouse after some of those bad outings, and he was completely shaken up. He'd say, 'What's wrong with me? I can't get anyone out, and my arm's killing me.' Doc talked very seriously about retiring. You hear that all the time from players, especially pitchers after bad games, but I'd never heard it from Doc. It hurt to listen to him talk like that. Actually, it was kind of shocking. A couple of times he'd come into the clubhouse after he'd gotten knocked out in the second or third inning and he'd tear the clubhouse apart, really throwing things around. I wouldn't have been surprised if Doc had retired after the ninety-four season. He wasn't coping very well with getting older."

The door was open for a relapse. What may have contributed to his downfall was major-league baseball's own lenience with him. After so many years of drug-free living, Gooden was no longer tested on the days he pitched, and by 1992 he was being tested only four times each half season. Furthermore, Gooden just about cut himself off from Alcoholics Anonymous meetings, pardoned by Dr. Lans because his attendance at such meetings was a distraction.

"That was the major thing, not having an aftercare program," Gooden said. "I don't care how strong you think you are, if you're an addict, you have to go to meetings." It was on June 2, 1994, that cocaine's demon reappeared in Gooden's life. He was in a Manhattan nightclub, drunk and continuing to drink. He was with friends, none of whom thought there was anything unusual about Doc being inebriated. After all, what better way for him to feel the self-pity of being injured, being a member of a bad team, and turning thirty than reaching for another cold one? Only, Gooden seemed to blink his eyes, and it was 3 A.M. The nightclub was closed now, and the only people left were a few employees, locking up. One who knew Gooden pulled out cocaine.

"Want some?" Gooden was asked.

Of course he did. The urge was there, thanks to the alcohol. There was no one there to stop him, not Dr. Lans, no fellow addicts, no teammates. Gooden was alone with his desire for the drug. Only for a fleeting second did he think about whether he'd get caught, but on an injury-rehab, and about to travel to Binghamton, New York, to pitch for the Mets' Double-A affiliate . . . who would possibly catch him up there? That decision-making process took all of a half second, in which time the cocaine had already invaded his system.

GOODEN WOKE UP the next day, and his first thought was a familiar one: panic. "I said to myself, 'What the fuck did I do?' " It had been seven years since he had last tested positive, and he was risking it all for . . . for what? There was no answer that could satisfy Gooden, only a sinking feeling that cocaine would forever haunt him.

"Doing it that one time made me aware, for the very first time, that once you're an addict, it can hit you again at any time," Gooden said. "There was no excuse for what I did, but all that heavy drinking, man, sooner or later it had to catch up with me."

Gooden was more than scared; he was paranoid. He pitched in Binghamton on Friday, June 3, his final start before coming off the disabled list, and spent the entire game checking the dugout to see if the representative from the testing agency would arrive. He didn't. Gooden then flew to Cincinnati on Saturday, June 4, to rejoin the Mets on their road trip, knowing that if he could get through one more day, then he'd be past the forty-eight-hour cutoff.

He stepped off the plane in Cincinnati, half expecting to see some Met official, or a testing rep, or even Acting Commissioner Bud Selig. Gooden was sweating now, his heart off on some kind of sprint. He went to the hotel, the minutes feeling like hours. And then Gooden went to Riverfront Stadium, where a rep was waiting. There he stood, smiling, pleasant as always, completely unaware of the panic within Gooden.

"Hi, Dwight," the rep said routinely. It had been like this for seven years, Gooden and some guy doing his job, the two of them making silly small talk while Doc went to the bathroom. Naturally, the guy would have to follow Gooden, and sometimes there would be a joke or two about that, but for the most part, Gooden was beyond feeling any embarrassment. It was the guy's job to watch, and it was Gooden's responsibility to produce a urine sample. After all, it was Gooden himself who was responsible for this scenario, not the other way around.

Only how was Gooden ever going to escape now? He considered just running for the door, pretending to be ill. Or maybe simply collapsing on the ground right there, clutching his chest and acting out a heart attack. Doc thought about simply saying no to the test. It took no more than five seconds for these possibilities to enter and leave Gooden's mind, and he rejected all of them as pointless. There was no running, no hiding. Gooden meekly said, "Let's go," and knew, on his way to the bathroom in the visitors' clubhouse, his only hope now was prayer.

Incredibly, two weeks elapsed between the time Gooden tested and the time the results came back. Two weeks, and every single day Gooden alternated between wild hope and his worst fears. During that time, he had returned from the disabled list and lost all three of his starts. On June 9, he was beaten 9–0 by the Expos. On June 14, he went down 3–2 to the Phillies, and on June 19, the final game he would win as a Met, Dwight Gooden defeated the Florida Marlins, 6–1. But the panic and prayer that kept churning inside of him:

Hope: There were no traces of coke found, he'd beaten the test.

Fear: He was caught, and baseball's executive council was meeting at that very moment.

Hope: The test had been lost somewhere in transit.

Fear: He would be banned for life.

Hope: He tested positive, but major-league baseball would be kind enough to look the other way.

Fear: He would be banned for life, never play again, never earn another dollar. The money would run out. He and his family would be destitute.

By the fourteenth day, Gooden had actually convinced himself that he'd escaped the crisis. Finally, on June 20 in Atlanta, Gooden stopped running.

It was Dr. Lans who delivered the news, having flown in from New York to do so. He was understandably grim.

"Dwight, I'm afraid we have a problem," Gooden recalled the doctor saying. "A test has come back positive. It's going to have to result in a suspension."

Gooden lowered his head as he learned the ramifications. He was to fly to New York to meet with officials from the Player Relations Committee and Players Association.

What could Gooden possibly tell his wife, Monica? The kids? Even more difficult, how would he explain the relapse to his mother, who had believed Dwight when he said the 1987 stay at Smithers had helped him beat cocaine? His recovery meant just as much as his career, and now . . . this.

"That was probably the hardest part of all, my mom," Gooden said. Her tears were almost too much for him to bear. For so long she believed her son was free of the drug's power. On June 24, the pitcher listened to the combined verdict from Gene Orza, the associate general counsel of the Players Association, and Lou Melendez, the associate council of the Player Relations Committee. There was very little either man could do for Gooden; they had to enforce the rules. And in this case, baseball was clear about second offenders: a mandatory sixty-day suspension without pay.

Gooden could live without two months' worth of paychecks. Unlike Strawberry, Doc had always saved and invested conservatively. Money wasn't the problem. The question was how to cope with another rehab stint, when, in truth, he was still in denial. Even until the last moments, as Gooden reached for the telephone to tell his mother, he thought of ways to keep the truth from her and from his friends. To all of them, Gooden said his suspension was due to the fact that he'd overslept when taking a nap and not made it to the clinic before it closed at 5 P.M., just as he claimed to have overslept in 1986 and missed the ticker-tape parade.

This time, Gooden simply said he missed a test, which in the eyes of major-league baseball is also a punishable offense for a player in recovery. "I was so sick, so deep into lying to myself, that I thought I could get my mother to believe it wasn't my fault, that all I did was skip a test," Gooden said. "I still didn't get it."

Neither did he understand why alcohol had brought him down, leading him right to cocaine. Gooden still didn't know how to stay away from the temptations that had—and would—derail such a promising baseball career. But before he could begin to fight his addiction, the Mets had one last request of Dr. K: would he pitch one last game, as scheduled?

"You want me to pitch? Are you serious?" Gooden asked McIlvaine. The general manager calmly tried to explain. According to a Met official, the request was made because "Dwight was still an active member of the team; the suspension hadn't taken effect yet. And to be honest, we didn't want to create a circus any sooner than necessary."

"They said the press would become suspicious," Gooden said, shaking his head. Suspicious of what? A news event that was about to spread in the next week anyway? What, exactly, did Gooden have to gain by pitching against the Pirates, except risk arm injury? Given the chance again, Gooden would never have stepped foot on the field. "There was no reason for me to pitch except to keep the Mets happy," Gooden said. It seemed he'd been doing that his whole career, and it made him angry to have been manipulated. "I thought it was very unfair of them," Gooden said in retrospect. On Friday, June 24, loyal and compliant to the end, Gooden made one final trip from the dugout to the pitching mound.

There was always something special about his windup, even in the grayer days of 1992 and 1993. Anyone who had had an inkling that Doc was about to end his association with the Mets might have paid closer attention to the enormous leg kick and the whiplike action of his arm. If ever there was a pitcher who generated power from his mechanics—unlike all-arm pitchers like Randy Johnson—it was Doc. When Gooden was in his prime in 1985, none other than Tom Seaver said it best: "Dwight has almost perfect mechanics."

June 24 turned out to be an awful night, "one of the worst of my career," Gooden said. Distracted and out of synch, he allowed nine runs, eight of them earned, in just five and a third innings. Doc walked off the mound in the sixth, head bowed, wanting to forget the moment as he left the dugout one last time. The Mets waited five more days to announce the bombshell of Gooden's fate, and while just about everyone expressed concern and shock, new manager Dallas Green took a surprisingly harsh view.

"Doc's problems are his own because he's an athlete who has fallen by the wayside by his own choice," Green said, although he was quick to say that he felt compassion for Gooden, then added, "I feel for the family." This was the first sign from the organization that it was distancing itself from the leftover relic from the eighties.

But Gooden was on the cover of the 1994 media guide because at the time he was their best, and maybe their only, goodwill ambassador. The Mets were just starting to rebuild from their stunning collapse under the Harazin-Torborg regime and had nothing else to offer fans except Doc's memories—the good ones, that is. But Gooden's contract was expiring at the end of the '94 season. Now it would be interesting to know what value McIlvaine attached to Gooden for '95 and beyond. "Now is not the time to ask those questions," McIlvaine said stiffly when someone did ask him about Gooden's future at Shea. Clearly, he was done.

Doc could forgive McIlvaine for not issuing him a vote of confidence. What else was the general manager going to say? That the Mets were going to welcome Gooden back for the possibility of a third failed test? The Mets were, and still are, one of the most publicity-conscious organizations in baseball, and they would have been sensitive to the message they would have been sending by allowing another Gooden comeback. This was harsh, especially because, in McIlvaine's words, "Dwight gave us flair." But that was then; this was the solemn burial of a pitcher who thought he'd beaten drugs but really hadn't.

On his way out, Gooden took note of Green's comments, remembering that "he buried me when I was down." In a way, it was possible to understand Green's distance from Doc. He didn't arrive at Shea until May 20, 1994, long after Gooden's reign over National League hitters had ended. Green never understood firsthand the hold Doc and his teammates had had on New Yorkers in the eighties, the feeling of arrogance they got from him, the assurance that if his start occurred in the middle of a winning streak, it was about to be extended. And if Doc pitched after the Mets had just lost, the losing streak was over.

Green said as much, observing, "I didn't see him pitch good. That's not saying a lot because he was on the disabled list part of nineteen ninety-three and again in ninety-four. But I didn't get a real shot at Doc. He had been up there for so many years, so far above it all, that all the little things didn't matter. He didn't need a change-up, he didn't need a slider, he didn't need to hold people on."

What Gooden needed on June 24, 1994, was help. The Mets released a statement from Doc in which he said: "I have been suspended for breaking the rules of my aftercare program. I'm truly sorry it happened. I want to apologize to the club, my teammates, and the people of New York City. I want to thank everyone for their past support. I will be back stronger and better. I want to earn your respect back."

Those were just words, pure spin, composed by the front office. Doc wasn't in the mood to thank anyone for anything; his world was spinning fast, and he needed help in regaining his equilibrium. As Gooden put it, "I couldn't even bring myself to read the papers. I didn't want to know what the press and everyone else was saying at that point."

Initially, the Mets had decided Gooden would return home to St. Petersburg, collect himself, and perhaps let the shock of his expulsion renew his efforts toward sobriety. Gooden met with his counselors, Drs. Robert Millman and Joel Solomon, who were attached to major-league baseball. Dr. Solomon was retained by the Players Association, and Dr. Millman's evaluations were commissioned by the clubs. Their recommendation was increased testing, not necessarily another stint in rehab. On July 1, 1994, Gooden flew to Tampa, spending his first summer at home since high school.

He was deeply depressed. That, and bored. For a man whose life had revolved around baseball for the last thirteen years, Gooden found the void too huge to comprehend. What did real people, especially unemployed ones, do with their lives? he wondered. Gooden would wake up in the morning and realize there was no reason to get out of bed. Florida was steamy-hot in July, the sun too oppressive even to go outside for a run or a game of basketball. And besides, Gooden thought, was it really worth it to be seen in public, to invite the stares, the side-of-the-mouth comments, even the pleasantries of well-wishers? Better to stay inside, find something to watch on the wide-screen TV.

Gooden had always been a loyal sports fan, especially devoted to the NFL and the Tampa Bay Buccaneers. But in the middle of the summer, baseball was everywhere on the tube. There was no hiding from it. How ironic that, on the day Gooden was supposed to have taken his next start at Shea, June 30, it rained.

It was the Fourth of July weekend when Gooden found himself at an outing, staring at a cold beer. Why not? he asked himself. Indeed, there was nothing between Doc and a case of beers if that's what he wanted. No game to pitch that night, no game the next night that would have been ruined by a hangover. Each day was a wide-open horizon now, and Gooden was free to create whatever reality he wanted.

But as in the past, one beer became six, then seven, and the next moment he would find himself gripping the steering wheel of his BMW, the engine thundering obediently at the touch of his foot. As if on autopilot, the car would steer itself onto the Howard Frankland Bridge to Tampa. The déjà vu washed all over Gooden; it was the winter of 1987 again, and all the old faces were there in front of him. The BMW would negotiate itself to the Belmont Heights section, where the drugs and, ultimately, Gooden's ruin were. Gooden would never actually cruise the streets of Tampa and have to roll down his window and cop. That was too crude a lifestyle. No, there were always "friends" who were ready to supply Doc, never asking questions, eager to make the man feel better about the awful turn his life had taken. And always, always, they found Gooden at night. "Something would always change in me after dark," he said. "It's like I became someone else, a vampire."

For three weeks, Gooden went on a binge he knew was out of control. "I couldn't stop. I was drinking just about every day, using, coming home so late my wife wouldn't even see me walking in the door," Gooden said. "Up to that point, I'd been in denial, but I knew it was time to get help."

All the while, baseball kept asking Gooden for drug tests, and he kept coming up dirty. One time, after he'd used, Gooden called Dr. Lans and asked if he should test anyway.

Lans advised him to do so. And that strengthened baseball's belief that Gooden's drug problem was out of control. And this time, not even Smithers would be entrusted with Doc's situation. Instead, Gooden flew to Palm Springs, California, on July 22, to the prestigious Betty Ford Clinic.

The grounds are set safely away from automobile traffic. Indeed, a patient can sense the clinic's tranquillity even in the short walk from the parking lot to the front door. Many, many celebrities have sought refuge at Betty Ford, and its most notable athlete in 1995 was Mickey Mantle, who emerged from the program saying the doctor's greatest breakthrough was getting him to write a letter to his deceased father. Mantle asked forgiveness for all the things he had never done for his dad, a guilt that, over the years, pushed him toward alcohol.

Gooden was given similar tools in understanding his own addiction. In many ways, the lessons he learned at the Betty Ford Clinic were the same ones that had been preached at Smithers: recognizing why he put himself in harm's way and why he continued to let alcohol be his bridge to drugs. As long as Gooden had even one beer, they told him, he was in danger. For twenty-eight days, Gooden worked with the finest counselors in the country and devoted himself to the most expensive program money could buy.

"It was a great place, a beautiful place, and inside, I felt great," Gooden said. "But let's face it, any rehab program is a piece of cake because you're protected there. The real test comes when you're tested, the very first time you get that urge and you're around people who are using, or you've been drinking. If you haven't made up your mind to change the people and places that were part of your world before, bam, it's going to hit you again. If you're still thinking you can do it your way, forget it."

The twenty-eight days came and went, and on the twenty-ninth, Gooden and his wife, Monica, were greeted at the clinic's doors by Darryl Strawberry. Almost a year later, their situations would be reversed, and it would be Gooden visiting Straw in Tampa while the outfielder was under house arrest. But now, in mid-August, it was Doc who needed the support.

After all, Strawberry had emerged from the very same clinic in June, just seventy-nine days earlier, and he looked healthy and refreshed. And he was quick with advice for Gooden. "Doc, you gotta get out of Florida, man," Darryl said. "It's not going to get any better for you unless you get away from those people."

That wasn't the first time Strawberry had attacked Tampa, but this time Darryl could at least say he'd left his old neighborhood. He and his new wife, Charisse, had moved to Rancho Mirage, just outside Palm Springs, a city surrounded by snow-capped mountains, so calm and beautiful Strawberry said, "I could live here the rest of my life." He walked Gooden around his ranch-style home, showed him the tennis courts in the backyard, then sat Gooden down in the living room and asked solemnly, "What are you gonna do now?"

"Try to get myself together, see if I can come back," Gooden said. The only trouble was, there was no baseball to return to, not at that point. The Players Association had called for a strike on August 12, interrupting Gooden's suspension with just fourteen days to go. The countdown could not continue until the labor dispute had been resolved. At least Strawberry had done his penance for his spring-training brush with coke and had hooked on with the San Francisco Giants, signing with them on June 20. But Gooden . . . well, the Mets hadn't said a word about his coming back, not even with two weeks to go on his suspension. Doc thought about that on the plane ride home to St. Petersburg. Just where was his baseball life heading? Did his fastball still have the octane necessary to cope with major-league hitters? Doc couldn't believe he was even asking the question. The fastball had been his life, his essence for so long. It was him, an extension of himself. And, Gooden realized, he'd taken a gift from God and nearly ruined it.

"In ninety-two and ninety-three, the drinking started to affect my performances," Gooden said. "It was a buildup, over a long time, but abusing your body will eventually catch up with you. I really couldn't hide from that fact anymore."

It took just three weeks for Gooden to undo the progress he'd made at Betty Ford, three weeks for the clinic's cocoon to be violated by Tampa's reality. Gooden was depressed, and, because he felt so low, he reached for a beer, then another, and then it was back to cocaine. A day or two later, the cycle would begin again. The urge was still there, as strong as it had ever been. Finally, Gooden was beginning to understand what the doctors had repeated so often at Smithers, that addiction stays for life. And it was equally obvious to Gooden that the drug had a powerful hold on him, especially now that he was so melancholy. Cocaine used to be a toy for celebration, used primarily when he was happy in the eighties. Now, older and sadder in the nineties, he found in cocaine a different kind of release—it made Doc forget that he was unemployed, no longer a star, years beyond his heyday.

"It was a way out," Gooden said, "although I knew in my heart using drugs wasn't fixing anything."

The Player Relations Committee in New York said test results were positive. Gooden was using cocaine again, and this time his usage was heavier than ever. Doc knew he would be caught, but not even the threat of further punishment acted as a deterrent. It was no longer a question of when Doc would be able to pitch again; there were officials who began to wonder if he would ever be coke-free. No one had forgotten the fate of pitcher Rod Scurry, a lefty with an enormous curveball and an even bigger appetite for cocaine. Scurry was a far better pitcher in his eight years with the Pirates, Yankees, and Mariners than his 19-32 record ever showed. But he, too, was sabotaged by cocaine. It ruined his career and, one day in 1992, killed him.

By mid-September 1994, Gooden was sending back too many positive tests to ignore, and the Mets made an unprecedented appeal to the commissioner's office. Please stop testing Dwight, owner Fred Wilpon asked. Stop, and let us test him ourselves. The Mets reasoned that it was almost pointless to continue since Doc seemed overwhelmed by the drug. Wilpon and McIlvaine promised to oversee Gooden's recovery personally, to set up their own testing program, even shoulder the expenses themselves. That way, the Mets could present Gooden to the executive council in however many months or years it would take to get him sober. But to keep testing now . . . well, Wilpon asked, why drive Gooden down even deeper?

Selig, members of the executive council, and PRC counsel Louis Melendez appreciated the sincerity of the Mets' request. But they vowed not to turn their backs on a still active player while he was suffering. One official said, "The idea of the tests wasn't to embarrass or humiliate Dwight, or push him down any deeper. It was our only way of knowing how serious the problem was." According to one person familiar with Gooden's test pattern, he tested positive at least eight times in the fall of 1994.

Gooden confesses that he was using coke freely but is quick to say, "A lot of those tests were showing traces from the same usage. I mean, I'd use on a Friday or Saturday, or even Sunday, and it'd be there in Monday's test, and sometimes in Wednesday's test, too," he said. "Not that it's any excuse, but I think they might've had the wrong idea about the number of times I did actually use."

Still, doctors were so baffled by Goodens's regression since leaving Betty Ford that they prescribed Prozac. But the antidepressant drug did nothing to stem the tide of positive tests, and Gooden conceded, "I still felt like I couldn't beat the thing. Prozac didn't do anything about the urges. I didn't want to talk to anyone, not even my wife and kids about it."

On September 15, the Mets were forced to announce that Gooden had tested positive, careful not to reveal the extent of his relapse. The club merely said Doc would not rejoin the team in 1994, although one club official said, "There was never really a plan in place to bring Dwight back in nineteen ninety-four. We were going to play it by ear and see how he did."

Once it became obvious the strike would wipe out the remainder of the '94 season, Gooden felt more hopeless than ever. He would take the BMW back and forth over the Howard Frankland Bridge, pushing the engine, testing the fates. He couldn't understand how, after seven years, he could still have been in coke's clutches so deeply. "No one ever beats this thing," Gooden said to himself. "Ever."

IT WAS EARLY one November morning in 1994 when Gooden walked in the door of his $3.5 million home. He had been using the night before, and just as he was getting in, cocaine was still in his system.

"Dwight, I'm taking the kids to school," his wife said from the kitchen, unaware of her husband's condition. Gooden was sitting on the couch in the living room and wanted to play with his children before they left, especially with his daughter Ashley. But he couldn't allow himself to get too close because he was still high.

Too drugged up for his own kids. Damn, Gooden thought, how much worse does it get? He found out that very day, when the mailman delivered a thin white envelope from Commissioner Bud Selig's desk. The message was one Gooden realized had been coming all along.

He knew what the punishment would be. He had been suspended twice, and that hadn't stopped him because Gooden always believed he could sober up in time for another season. There would always be another season, another chance. But not now.

Selig told Gooden, and agent Jim Neader in a carbon-copy letter delivered the same day, that he would be suspended for one year for repeated violations of his aftercare program. There would be no baseball in 1995. Alone in the house, and even more alone with his depression, Gooden at least had the clarity of mind to understand that he faced two choices.

"I either get my life together right now," he said. "Or else I'm gonna be dead soon."

A SECOND CHANCE

DARRYL STRAWBERRY LOOKED rested, sounded clearheaded, and, as always, still had only 6.2 percent body fat—a frame body so chiseled the Mets used to say it resembled a washboard.

Only it wasn't the Mets who were admiring Strawberry this time around. It was his new employers, the San Francisco Giants, who scooped up Strawberry out of the Betty Ford Clinic and, on June 20, 1994, signed him to a partial-year contract. It was a marriage of convenience: the Giants were nine games under .500 and losers of twenty-three of their last thirty-three games, and Strawberry needed a job.

Since he'd left the Betty Ford Clinic, Strawberry had talked to the Padres and flirted with the Expos, but it was the Giants who intrigued him most. He said, "I liked the idea of being in the same division with the Dodgers." There was plenty of happy talk about harboring no hard feelings, especially toward Tommy Lasorda, but there was enough pride in Strawberry to want the last word.

Certainly, the Giants were ready to believe that. On Monday, June 17, Strawberry met for four hours with Giants president Peter Magowan, executive vice president Larry Baer, manager Dusty Baker, and hitting instructor Bobby Bonds. He talked, they listened, they asked, he answered. The Giants were clearly concerned about whether Strawberry could still play; after all, he was thirty-two and hadn't swung a bat in over a year. But mostly they wanted to know about Strawberry's head. Was he ready to live a drug-free life?

Giving Strawberry another chance wasn't an easy choice for the Giants. Indeed, many general managers in the baseball community were ready to give up on him. But Magowan felt the sincerity of Strawberry's appeal and was impressed with his family's unique offer: as a guarantee of his sobriety, Darryl would bring his brother Michael as a traveling companion/bodyguard and pay him out of his own pocket.

Magowan nodded in approval, saying, "It seemed like a solution that would work." It made sense all around: who knew Strawberry better than his brother, who not only understood Darryl's internal demons but those of the outside world, too? Michael Strawberry had been a member of the Los Angeles Police Department for ten years, assigned to a gang detail in South-Central L.A. During the Rodney King riots in May of 1992, Michael Strawberry and his partners came under fire from a rooftop ambush and Strawberry was grazed in the back of the head by a bullet from an AK-47. The gunman, a member of the 8-Trey gang, was convicted and sentenced to seventeen years to life.

The elder Strawberry had since retired from active duty in the LAPD and was assigned to reserve duty. In the meantime, he had become an ordained minister in the Blood Covenant Christian Faith Church in Pomona, California, and spent a week with Darryl during his stay at the Betty Ford Clinic. As part of the working agreement with the Giants, the club would pay Michael's traveling expenses and a stipend and Darryl would pay his brother the equivalent of a policeman's salary. Michael had predicted success with the experiment because, he recalled, "I always had a sixth sense about things. Being a police officer, I encountered a lot of things . . . now Darryl is playing with a clear head and clean conscience."

At age thirty-two, Strawberry's life had finally taken a better path. No matter that the Giants' desire to employ Michael implied a certain lack of trust—at least there was another chance for Darryl. Bobby Bonds said, "What I saw and heard from Darryl told me he was ready. He made mistakes, but we all believed that he deserved another shot."

Strawberry would be working for one of the loosest, and certainly hippest, managers in baseball in Dusty Baker. It's been said that if a player cannot serve Baker, then he doesn't belong in the big leagues. Davey Johnson might have been too consumed with neutralizing Darryl's ego to help him, and Lasorda might have been too distant, but Baker offered the better qualities of both men. Like Davey, Dusty could be tough, and like Lasorda, Baker knew how to motivate. All the Giants asked was that Strawberry remain drug-free. Any relapse whatsoever and their agreement would terminate immediately.

It was Bobby Bonds who forged the closest relationship with Darryl, becoming the successor in a long line of father figures. Perhaps the connection had something to do with Bonds's own understanding of being a superstar, as he had played on the same Giants teams in the sixties as Willie Mays and Willie McCovey. Although not the most devastating hitter of his time, Bonds was certainly among the elite, having slugged 332 home runs in his fourteen-year career, six times surpassing thirty homers in a season.

Darryl soon went as far as to say Bonds was his "best friend" among the Giants. "He was someone I loved talking to, about everything. He was all around a good guy. I came to trust him a lot," Strawberry said. Bobby was also the father of the game's greatest hitter in the early nineties. But there was more to Barry Bonds than his bat speed; he had the greatest, most outrageous ego of any player in the National League, possibly in all of baseball. Reporters could find Barry both delightful and arrogant in the same interview, but his ego actually made it easier for Strawberry to assimilate in the Giants clubhouse, just as Barry had been the perfect shield for Bobby Bonilla with the Pirates five years earlier.

For once, Darryl wasn't the most boastful player in the clubhouse. In fact, Darryl appeared wise, even humble, in contrast to Barry Bonds. For his part, Bonds was more than happy to accept Strawberry because Darryl still intimidated pitchers, and that meant Bonds was seeing fatter, middle-of-the-plate fastballs.

Barry Bonds said that upon Strawberry's arrival, "I was challenged more than anytime I was in the majors. They can't pitch around me much. It's fun."

On his very first day back, July 7, Strawberry arrived from Phoenix, where he had been training with the Giants' Triple-A affiliate, took a cab from the airport to Candlestick Park, and walked into the clubhouse at 8:30 A.M., a full four hours before game time. Strawberry didn't get a hit in a 5–4 win over the Phillies but did draw an intentional walk in the eighth inning from Larry Andersen, a remarkable show of respect for a player so rusty.

The Phillies had already learned plenty about Strawberry in the sixth inning, when he drove a monstrous blast to dead center. Had Milt Thompson not made a graceful, leaping catch at the wall, Strawberry would have homered to the deepest part of the stadium. Phillies right-hander Shawn Boskie, who delivered the near home run, said, "It was amazing to watch. I had a lot of fun just watching Darryl; he still has great bat speed. Not many guys can hit a ball into the wind to dead central. He hits the ball to left, and it's over the bleachers."

With Strawberry in the lineup, both Barry Bonds and the Giants prospered. Bonds went on a fourteen-for-thirty-one streak (.451) with eleven RBIs. The Giants, meanwhile, won nine straight and inched to within three and a half games of the division-leading Dodgers. The strike interrupted whatever plans the Giants had of capturing the West in '94, but they were left with a fine impression of Strawberry's recovery: he didn't show any signs of a relapse, and with him in the lineup they were 19-10. Although Strawberry's overall numbers weren't overwhelming in themselves—.239, four home runs, seventeen RBIs in ninety-two at-bats—there were enough flashes of greatness for the Giants to offer him arbitration that November. That meant Strawberry was guaranteed a job for 1995 or whenever the strike ended.

But there was other trouble on the horizon for Strawberry. The Internal Revenue Service had been investigating him since 1992 for failing to report income from card shows. At the height of their success in the mid- to late eighties, many Mets could make hundreds of thousands of dollars by appearing at such shows—which offered the public face-to-face contact with their heroes in a setting more intimate than the ballpark. Strawberry, for instance, had such drawing power he could sign a thousand autographs for fifteen dollars apiece in a three-hour session. The $15,000 would invariably be paid in cash, and it wasn't unusual to see Met players walking away from these shows—held throughout the metropolitan area, from Atlantic City all the way to the tip of Long Island—with swollen paper bags in their hands.

The Strawberry-autographed card or baseball could then be resold on the black market. Depending on the popularity of a player, a single autograph, like Joe DiMaggio's, could command as much as $175. Before his death, Mickey Mantle's name meant $85 (now it is worth over $100), Reggie Jackson's $45, Hank Aaron's $45, Pete Rose's $25, and on and on.

Of course, there was no law against making extra money this way. It was a perk of big-league life—easy cash, walking-around dollars, currency that could translate into an extra Rolex or a Mercedes. The problem was whether that money was reported to the IRS. Even for some players with million-dollar salaries, the temptation to pocket the extra thousands was too much.

The investigation began with a 1992 subpoena of a thirty-two-year-old card-show broker named Meade Chasky. Chasky, who weighed nearly four hundred pounds, was a recognizable figure in the Met clubhouse. With the exception of Roger McDowell, Jesse Orosco, Mookie Wilson, and Bobby Ojeda—who distrusted Chasky and said so openly—Chasky had ties to virtually every player in the clubhouse. "He was the money man," said equipment manager Charlie Samuels, which is why Met management was so distrustful of him.

General Manager Frank Cashen repeatedly warned the Mets to stay away from Chasky. "He's going to go down one day" was how one Met remembered Cashen's prediction. "The IRS is going to get him, and he'll take you all with him." One club official dismissed Chasky as just "a glorified go-fer who would practically do the players' laundry just to keep his contacts." Yet, ironically, it was the cleanest Met of all, Gary Carter, who introduced Chasky to the Mets' opulence. Chasky, a Queens native, was introduced to Carter by Duke Snider when he was a member of the Montreal Expos. Chasky's father had been a longtime Brooklyn Dodgers fan and befriended Snider when he was a Montreal broadcaster.

From Snider to Carter, then Tim Raines and Andre Dawson, Chasky won the Expos' trust, and when Carter was traded to New York before the 1985 season, he brought Meade with him into the clubhouse. While it was true that Chasky sometimes acted as a personal valet, picking up players at airports and chauffeuring them in and out of Manhattan, it was soon apparent he was the Mets' conduit to thousands in card-show money.

It was Chasky's job to find card-show promoters and then produce the players. He was the classic middleman and aptly called his first enterprise The Appearance Man. Eventually, Chasky's business flourished under a company name: Prime Time Sports Marketing, and, at the height of the golden era at Shea, Chasky easily cleared $125,000 a year. Carter said, "We made so much money in those days, it was scary." Yet, the IRS's initial investigation yielded no criminal wrongdoing on Chasky's part; indeed, it found copies of 1099 forms for each of his invoices. But the Feds were particularly interested in the Mets who profited from Chasky's business or, as he put it, "the ones who I made rich."

The list included Strawberry, Gooden, Carter, Lenny Dykstra, Keith Hernandez, and Ron Darling. The IRS learned almost instantly that Carter was as honest with his taxes as he was in every other area of his life. When he was subpoenaed before a grand jury in White Plains, New York, Carter spent nearly $25,000 in accountants' fees to produce every invoice and receipt from his card-show appearances and walked away knowing, "There was nothing the U.S. Attorney's office was ever going to be able to question me about."

But that wasn't the case with Strawberry. Chasky sensed trouble was on the way for Darryl, whom he still considered a friend. "We used to go out all the time in the eighties. I was there some of the times when Darryl had done his share of drinking," Chasky said. "I had a feeling Darryl was cheating on his taxes to some extent. He'd say, 'Fuck the IRS, it's my money, I'll do what I want with it.' "

Strawberry came to New York in the fall of 1992 with the Dodgers, and at that time Chasky warned him the IRS investigation would soon turn its attention to him. According to Chasky, Strawberry said, "Get your lawyer on the phone and have him call me." In a subsequent conversation, Strawberry offered to fly Chasky and his lawyer, Michael Salnick, to Los Angeles at his own expense to meet with Strawberry's agent, Eric Goldschmidt, who was also a certified public accountant.

After the '92 season, Chasky and Salnick did fly to the West Coast, where they met with Goldschmidt. But Strawberry never showed up, which Chasky found unusual, nor did he ever reimburse the promoter for his costs. That, Chasky said, was not out of character.

"Darryl was never very good with money. I was always lending it to him," he said. "To be honest, Darryl was always broke, never able to pay his mortgage, always in over his head with American Express. I'd say over the years, I had to have loaned him somewhere between thirty and forty thousand dollars. I did it, though. I did it because I liked Darryl. I'll give you an example: when he was going into Smithers in nineteen ninety, he sold me his World Series ring and said, 'I don't want it anymore. Fuck the Mets. I hate them.' I paid him ten thousand dollars for it. When Darryl got out, he'd changed his mind, both about the Mets and the ring. He decided he wanted it back. I sold it right back to him for the ten thousand dollars. I could've easily sold it elsewhere and made a profit for myself or even sold it back to Darryl and made a profit on him. But I couldn't have done that, not to him. I considered myself loyal to him."

But their friendship ended the next spring, when Chasky visited Strawberry at the Dodgers' camp in Vero Beach, Florida. He found the outfielder not only uncommunicative but hostile as well. "Darryl thought I ratted him out," Chasky said. "And we've never spoken again. I used to like him, but the way I feel about him now, the way he's gone around blaming me, calling me a rat, ruining my reputation and hurting my business, I wouldn't even bother to piss on him."

Although Strawberry had heard the IRS was now moving against him, apparently he was unaware of the long-range consequences. When reporters asked him about the investigation, Strawberry flippantly said, "The Feds can kiss my ass." That only strengthened their resolve to bring him down, and Strawberry admitted later, "I wish I hadn't said that. It wasn't right. But I had no idea what the investigation was about, and I just didn't take it seriously."

Strawberry tried to put the IRS out of his mind for the duration of the '93 and '94 seasons, but the agency was relentless in its pursuit. In the spring of '94, there were rumors throughout baseball that Strawberry had become a government informant, that he had even turned on his buddy Gooden.

Strawberry still denies this charge, claiming, "There's no way in the world I would ever take down another player.

That's not the kind of person I am." But Carter was told by prosecutors the reason so many Mets were being investigated was because of Strawberry's willingness to expose them.

"The lawyers for the prosecution said Darryl told them, 'If I'm going down, there were a lot of players doing the same thing.' " Carter said. "That's the way it was explained to me. I don't know about the other guys, but I know that because of Darryl I had to spend a lot of time and effort clearing my name."

Chasky and Carter agreed on this much: neither one considered Strawberry a criminal. His worst crime may have been his ignorance of the law. Carter said, "Trust me, Darryl had no idea what he was headed into." Chasky said, "I think he got bad advice, that's all, about what it meant not to pay taxes." Even a member of Strawberry's family said, "Darryl just isn't sophisticated enough to have some elaborate scheme and conspiracy against the government."

To what degree that might have been true, all the IRS was interested in was the signature on the bottom of Strawberry's tax forms, which indicated his responsibility for them. Darryl claimed, "I never did anything to hurt anyone, except myself." And that point never became more vivid than on December 9, 1994.

AFTER NEARLY THREE years of investigation, a federal grand jury in White Plains charged Strawberry and Eric Goldschmidt with one count of income-tax conspiracy and two counts of tax evasion. The indictment charged that Strawberry and Goldschmidt, who had helped him prepare his returns, failed to pay $146,000 in income taxes between 1986 and 1990. The possible punishment included five years in jail and a $250,000 fine or twice the gross amount owed to the government, whichever was greater. According to the investigation, Strawberry hid an estimated $502,043 of the $945,000 he made from promotions in a Queens bank account.

As dark a day as it was for baseball, Strawberry certainly wasn't the first to go down on tax charges. In 1990, Pete Rose had been sentenced to five months in a federal penitentiary after pleading guilty to tax evasion and was fined $50,000. Strawberry strongly defended himself to members of the press, saying that it was either Goldschmidt or Chasky, or both, who were guilty of tax fraud, although subsequently both men were cleared of such charges.

"All I ever did was sign the forms that were put in front of me at the end of the year," Strawberry said. "I have no idea what Eric was doing or why. I don't know if Meade was giving Eric the wrong information or Eric was doing something wrong, but it's wrong what's happening to me. I trusted a lot of people who, it turned out, wanted to take me down."

Although the Giants said they remained committed to Strawberry—General Manager Bob Quinn said the club had no intention of taking disciplinary action against their embattled outfielder—Acting Commissioner Bud Selig called the indictment "a sad day for baseball."

Strawberry contemplated going to trial to clear his name, and for a while his attorneys talked tough. John Tigue, Jr., said, "Darryl denies that charge, and he hopes to have a trial schedule which will permit him to participate fully in the nineteen ninety-five season, if there is one." But behind the scenes, Strawberry's legal team was working to ease the pain of the irrefutable evidence against him. The government's determination was supplied by a tough assistant U.S. attorney named Carol Sipperly, who was affable and quick-witted in public but, behind closed doors, told her staff the government would make an example of Strawberry. If there was any plea bargain involved, it would have to involve jail time. Sipperly refused to relent on that.

For weeks, Martin Gelfand, Strawberry's lead attorney, negotiated with Sipperly about other options, including fines, community service, and a lengthy and severe probation. All Strawberry asked was that he be spared jail. Finally, on January 16, he received a phone call from Gelfand, relaying devastating news: the best he could squeeze from Sipperly was three months in a federal prison.

Strawberry put the phone down. He was alone in his home in Rancho Mirage, as his wife, Charisse, and their two children were visiting her parents in Encino. So Strawberry was left to wrestle with his failures by himself. Darryl accepted the blame for the incidents of domestic violence; he knew striking Lisa had been wrong, a result of his own addictions. Fighting Keith Hernandez in public was an embarrassment to this day. Alcohol and drugs were demons, and he swore never to touch either one again. Now he was staring at charges of tax evasion.

Strawberry took a deep breath and thought about how long ago 1983, when he was just a rookie with a long swing, able to send a fastball to the planets, seemed. New York was fun and innocent then; coming to Shea meant playing baseball with friends in front of warm and sympathetic crowds. So much had gone wrong since then, and, at that moment, Darryl was very, very tired.

Tired of saying the wrong thing, tired of making the wrong decisions, tired of trusting selfish people, tired of the headlines that always, always followed. It was true, Strawberry loved publicity; it's what made him a better ballplayer because he liked challenges. But did it have to hurt this much? Had he been so misguided in his life that he deserved to go to jail?

"I looked at myself in the mirror that day and said to myself, 'Man, I've done some fucked-up things, but am I really a criminal? Is that how far I've fallen?' " Strawberry said. "I just couldn't accept it . . . the whole idea of being in jail, behind bars, losing my freedom. All I ever tried to do was play baseball, be nice to fans, have some fun. Jail . . . man, I couldn't accept that."

Strawberry had heard stories about jail. Who hadn't? No matter that Strawberry was headed for the relative comfort of a federal prison, not a state penitentiary, where the more violent criminals were housed. Jail was still jail, and, as he sat alone in his home, Strawberry considered his options.

Of course, he could refuse the offer and go to trial. But Gelfand warned Strawberry of the risk involved: if convicted, he was almost certain to spend at least eighteen months behind bars. That would wipe out two full seasons and mean Strawberry would be thirty-five before he could return to the big leagues. By then, who knows what skills he would have had left, especially after being in prison for so long? And who would have given Strawberry a chance?

But if eighteen months was unacceptable to the baseball community, why would three months be any different? Either way, Strawberry would still be a convicted felon the rest of his life. And even if he was gone for only one day, it would mean another day of financial worry: Strawberry's legal costs were already overwhelming, as was the burden of spousal support for Lisa.

There was one other solution, and Strawberry couldn't deny the thought that kept running through his mind. Once before, in 1993, Strawberry had considered simply taking his life. It was in his worst days with the Dodgers, when the fans were booing him and he found out General Manager Fred Claire had put him on waivers. Despite the bargain-basement price of $20,000, no team had claimed Strawberry. "That hurt a lot. I didn't even want to go back to the Dodgers after that, having them think I was just taking their money. So, yeah, I thought about what it would be like if I wasn't around anymore," Strawberry said. "Then people wouldn't have anything to talk about."

Now, in 1995, Strawberry was edging closer to a similar cliff. Looking down, there was nothing but darkness. "It was there, the thought about killing myself," he said. If it was going to happen, Strawberry decided he'd get high first. He poured himself a drink; one, then another, and then a third. Soon he was drunk. Funny how fast the cocaine appeared in front of Strawberry. He'd had it with him, even though it had been eight months since he had last used. He thought the urges were finally evaporating. But now . . . why not, he thought.

Strawberry did a line, then two, and then a few more. But strangely, the cocaine didn't feel as exhilarating as he'd imagined. In fact, Strawberry realized his desire to end his life was foolish and, considering the pain he'd cause his family, extremely selfish. He got up, walked to the bathroom, and flushed the cocaine down the toilet, not quite comprehending that his career was close behind.

"I HAD A little slipup," Strawberry told a reporter on the telephone the next day. "It was a little thing. I'm going to be all right. It was my mistake."

Strawberry was right about that. Using cocaine on January 14 didn't alleviate his problems with the IRS, but it certainly created trouble with major-league baseball. Strawberry knew he would fail the ensuing drug tests, but there was no hiding from them. Within two weeks, Strawberry's brief but promising comeback with the Giants was over. He was released by the club for violating his aftercare program. Four days after that, Strawberry was suspended by the commissioner for sixty days, and, following that, he pleaded guilty to tax evasion.

It was a dizzying pace of events, even by Strawberry's hectic standards. But somewhere, in the last few weeks of January, he'd found peace with the path he'd chosen. He'd had long talks with his wife, his brothers, his mother. Darryl once again found comfort in the church. He'd made up his mind that being punished would allow him to act as a role model, albeit a flawed one, as long as he remained clean the rest of his life.

"I made up my mind that I was gonna do the time, make it as painless as possible, and then get on with my life," Strawberry said. "The thing with the IRS was hanging over my head for so long . . . it was such a tremendous weight to me and my wife, my entire family. At least I was gonna get the three months out of the way, then get my career back on track. I knew there were teams out there that wanted me."

It was the old Strawberry-speak, full of confidence and tough talk. If there was ever a rock that Darryl leaned on, it was his ability to hit a fastball, which, he learned in 1994, hadn't deserted him. As for the embarrassment of jail time . . . well, it was his friend Eric Davis who put it best, saying, "It takes a lot to humiliate Darryl. He's strong in that way. He can take the public exposure, even when it's bad."

The days leading up to the appearance in federal court were slow and comfortable for Strawberry. He was enjoying his new home on Bob Hope Drive in Rancho Mirage, purchased for

$1.2 million in July 1994, right after his release from the
Betty Ford Clinic. It was nearly 5,700 square feet, and its
sunken tennis court was framed by African sumac trees.

"Come on, let's go for a drive," he said to a visiting news-
paper reporter. The two slipped into his Mercedes 500 and
cruised slowly through downtown Palm Springs. Actually,
Strawberry was on his way to his three-times-a-week drug
test, a routine that was never interrupted, not even with the
recent relapse. "Taking my tests, staying clean. That slipup is
never going to happen again," he said. "I'm not the kind
of addict who has a day-to-day urge anymore. I'm past that
now. I know I still have to go to meetings, but my problem
was the pressure . . . the IRS, jail, and all that. I'm gonna
be fine."

It was then that Strawberry was delivered an unusual message. It was from former heavyweight contender Gerry Cooney,
himself a recovering addict and in town to lecture at the Betty
Ford Clinic. Cooney was one of the biggest names in boxing in
the early eighties, a great white hope who wasn't ready for the
hype—or the title shot he got in 1982 against Larry Holmes.
Although he nearly knocked Holmes out in the tenth round,
Cooney was TKOed in the thirteenth and succumbed to a
postfight depression so deep it led to drug addiction.

For six years, Cooney battled cocaine and even fought under
the influence of the drug Percodan during a comeback bout
against George Chaplin. Cooney finally ended his career in
1990, getting knocked out in the second round by George
Foreman, and he later said, "That was best thing I ever did for
myself. I trained and fought clean, and I got knocked out. It
was a sign to walk away."

Now Cooney was trying to help other addicts, and he saw
parallels between his career and Strawberry's. When Darryl

heard the ex-boxer was looking for him, he made a call right from his car phone.

"Gerry, this is Darryl Strawberry. I'm getting back to you."

"Darryl, man, I'm glad you called. You know I've been a big fan of yours for a long time. How are you?"

"I'm hanging in there."

"Yeah, I hear things have been a little rough for you. Look, I'm speaking at the clinic tomorrow night. I'd love it if you could make it. You think you can come?"

"Yeah, Gerry. I'll see if I can."

"That'd be great, man. Look, Darryl, I know everyone in the world is in your ear, wanting a piece of you. I was there myself. Just don't do what I did. I was at the top, and I threw it away. I just wanted to get away from the noise. My world was moving so fast, I wanted to stop and get off. I mean, I really didn't give a shit."

"I know what you mean, Gerry. Sometimes I wonder why it's no fun anymore."

"You got another chance. You can't keep asking for more chances. Treat this one like it's your last, Darryl. Don't throw it away, okay? I'm telling you as someone who's been there."

"I appreciate that."

"Darryl, am I gonna see you tomorrow?"

"I'll be there."

The next night, Cooney spoke to a roomful of addicts at the clinic. Strawberry did not attend.

THE FEDERAL COURTHOUSE on White Plains Road was surrounded by members of the press, and it was hardly a secret for whom they were waiting. It was April 25, Judgment Day for Strawberry, who stood before the government and awaited sentencing. Darryl arrived via limousine at 1 P.M., sharply dressed, although outfitted with an outrageous purple tie—

after having flown in from Los Angeles and spending the night at a hotel in White Plains. With Strawberry was Charisse, now seven months pregnant, his two lawyers, Martin Gelfand and Jack Tigue—tax specialists who had long since replaced Bob Shapiro—as well as his new agent, Bill Goodstein. Goodstein had been retained a month earlier, entrusted primarily with the chore of finding Strawberry work in the big leagues again.

At 11 A.M., Strawberry called Gooden at home in St. Petersburg and told him, "Don't worry, I would never do anything to hurt you." Even until the last moments, there were Mets who feared that a jail-bound Darryl would take them down. The rumors were so persistent, and so deeply troubled Strawberry, he decided to address the issue directly with Gooden. Darryl wanted Doc to have peace of mind, no matter how his sentencing turned out. Doc laughed and said the possibility of being betrayed had never crossed his mind, which may or may not have been a white lie. Having made his peace with an old buddy, Strawberry walked into Room 401 and braced for the worst.

A half hour or so before the proceedings began, Strawberry, his attorneys, and Assistant U.S. Attorney Sipperly met in Judge Barrington Parker's chambers, and the discussion was far beyond whether Darryl would do jail time. The lawyers only argued when and where. Gelfand asked for a prison assignment close to Southern California so he would be close to his family. Gelfand further asked if Strawberry could at least complete his jail term after the baseball season.

"Standing right there, listening to all that, I was fully prepared to go to jail," Strawberry said. "I arranged it in my mind that the worst was going to happen. After a while, you can't keep taking all that weight. You just say to yourself, 'Whatever happens, happens. Time to get on with my life.' "

Yet Goodstein whispered an odd prediction into Strawberry's ear moments before heading into the courtroom. "Don't worry, Darryl, you're not going to spend a single hour in jail," said Goodstein, himself a lawyer. "Thanks, Bill," Strawberry said, although he immediately dismissed Goodstein's counsel as a last-minute pick-me-up.

The courtroom was packed with reporters and a few stragglers awaiting other legal business after Strawberry's. Sipperly and her assistants sat at a table to the judge's right, and Strawberry, Gelfand, Tigue, and Goodstein sat to Parker's left. Sipperly herself was several months' pregnant and, turning to Charisse Strawberry, pleasantly asked, "How are you?"

"Fine," Mrs. Strawberry said through a forced smile and under her breath mumbled, "Great. Now, she's nice."

Gelfand went first, asking Judge Parker for leniency for Strawberry. The lawyer argued that Darryl be allowed to play baseball immediately.

"If he is gainfully employed, Your Honor, then Mr. Strawberry can support his family, he can pay back taxes, and he can establish his market value as a major-league player," Gelfand said. "And furthermore, Your Honor, Mr. Strawberry is on the cusp of being drug-free for the rest of his life. We ask you to remember that Meade Chasky, the architect of this scheme, has been granted total immunity . . . Darryl Strawberry is just one individual in hundreds of card shows. We don't believe the government should make Mr. Strawberry the sole measure of deterrence. He has a short career as a professional athlete. We ask that he be allowed to pursue it. And in regards to a jail sentence, we ask for some consideration as to his assignment."

Then it was Sipperly's turn, and she showed just how tough she'd been all along. Small and compact, with a raspy voice, Sipperly told Judge Parker there was no reason why Strawberry shouldn't surrender to federal authorities within two to four weeks, bluntly noting that not only did Strawberry fail a recent drug test but that he had no job, either.

"There's a difference, Your Honor, between potential for employment and being gainfully employed," Sipperly said. "Furthermore, Mr. Chasky was never granted any immunity whatsoever."

She then turned to Gelfand and said, "And counsel knows prison assignments are not the responsibility of the court but of the Bureau of Prisons."

Strawberry listened to the proceedings impassively, his huge shoulders slumped slightly forward. If he was nervous, or angry with Sipperly, or on the verge of tears, he didn't show it. In fact, Strawberry was surprisingly eloquent as he took his turn before Judge Parker.

"Your Honor, I take full responsibility for the mess I've caused myself and my family," he said. "I got poor advice, and if I'd understood what I'd been doing all these years, then I wouldn't be in this situation today. As for my recent slipup with drugs, it was the first time in my life that I've been afraid for my life. The idea of going to jail was very difficult for me to deal with, especially since my wife is pregnant. Not being available for my family, not being there, I started to ask myself, 'Is it all worth it?' "

Strawberry sat down and awaited sentencing. It was a foregone conclusion that Judge Parker would abide by the government's recommendation, especially since the plea bargain specifically called for a three-month jail term. The only suspense was finding out how soon Strawberry would be sent to prison and where.

Charisse Strawberry started crying softly to herself. "I think I'm going into labor right now," she said as Parker began. His voice was deep, his words slow. With eyes closed, it was possible to believe Darth Vader was presiding over the court.

"It's obvious to everyone that you had extraordinary gifts and abilities, but you have shown an egregious lack of judgment and a puzzling immaturity in evading over one hundred thousand dollars in taxes," Parker said, staring directly at Strawberry. "I am not unmindful of the fact that although you have taken steps to shorten your career, you do have time left. What has influenced me most today is that you before the court have pled guilty to a felony. We live in a society where the stigma of a felony is not easily erased. Barring an unlikely turn of events, it's likely you will carry that stigma with you to your grave."

At that point, Sipperly's face tightened like a fist. Charisse Strawberry whispered to a friend, "What does this all mean?" And Strawberry's lawyers leaned forward in their chairs, not quite sure they could believe their ears.

Parker calmly then dropped his bombshell on the court: he sentenced Strawberry to three years' probation, six months' home confinement, one hundred hours of community service, and $350,000 in back taxes. For all the government's efforts to crush Strawberry—for all its threats to put him away for two years and possibly end his career—not only did Strawberry beat a prison sentence but he wasn't even hit with court fines.

Sipperly lowered her head in disbelief as Strawberry turned and hugged his wife. Charisse was crying into his shoulder, and, for a moment, it appeared Darryl would break down, too. Parker warned Strawberry, "Your future is in your hands now." Once again, Strawberry had been given another chance.

LONG AFTER THE court had emptied, Sipperly was waiting for an elevator on her way out of the building. She looked tired and, to a degree, still stunned. Sipperly smiled sadly when asked about Parker's sentence. "I have nothing to say. It's the judge's decision," she said quietly.

Not surprisingly, U.S. Attorney Mary Jo White said she was "disappointed" in Parker, reminding the judge that "prison sentences are appropriate for violators of the tax laws in order to deter others from attempting to evade paying their fair share of taxes." A spokesman for White went even further, saying, "No matter what Darryl said about getting bad advice, he knew what he was doing. No one pleads guilty unless they are, in fact, guilty."

Then what, exactly, was Parker thinking? Mike Lupica wrote the next day in *Newsday,* "We live in an age when people are amazed when someone such as Pete Rose or Mike Tyson actually does time. More and more, people believe there is one justice for the rich and famous and another kind of justice, much less forgiving."

Parker's private explanation wasn't any different from the one he delivered in his courtroom. "Ultimately, it's my decision about sentencing, not the prosecution's," he said. "And I felt in this case, the fact that Mr. Strawberry would have to continue as a professional athlete, in the public arena, with the tag of a convicted felon, was significant penalty, as well as a deterrent."

A few miles away at a Stouffer's hotel, Strawberry, Charisse, and Bill Goodstein enjoyed a quiet celebration over lunch.

"You realize what a wonderful second chance you've gotten, don't you, Darryl?" Goodstein asked.

"I know, I really do. It's a blessed day," Strawberry said. "It's a huge weight off my shoulders. At least I can get on with my life, show people that I have reformed. I'm very, very thankful I've been given another chance."

At the very worst, Strawberry would be back in baseball by June 26, and he promised his first order of business would be "payback, starting with Tommy Lasorda." The Dodger manager's hard-line stand on Strawberry was one thing; everyone was entitled to an opinion about drug addiction. But what really angered Darryl was being compared unfavorably to a dog by Lasorda.

"At least a dog will run after a ball," Lasorda had said bitterly. "He's a sick guy," Strawberry said in response. Oh, how he would have loved to walk into Dodger Stadium sometime in late September and hit a five-hundred-foot home run to break Lasorda's spirit. If Strawberry had any choice in the matter, he would have returned to the Giants because he felt so close to Bobby Bonds and Dusty Baker. At least Giants owner Peter Magowan sounded sympathetic to Darryl, saying, "It certainly helps him a great deal that there's no jail time involved."

But a high-ranking member of the Giants' organization asked, "What kind of message would we be sending our fans if we let Darryl come back after he'd failed a drug test and after he'd pleaded guilty to a tax-evasion felony? We have to be sensitive to our public."

No one argued that Strawberry could still hit. And he was certainly in shape. But who wanted to take a chance on him? Suddenly, the most important figure in Strawberry's life became his new agent, Goodstein. A New York lawyer with strong political connections in Manhattan—he served as special counsel to the Mollen Commission, which investigated corruption in the New York City Police Department—the fifty-four-year-old Goodstein had a long but curiously limited career as a baseball agent. Although he'd had relationships with Reggie Jackson and Willie Randolph in the seventies, Goodstein forged his reputation primarily with Dave Righetti and was at the center of the Yankee universe with him when Righetti was at his peak, leading the American League in saves with forty-six in 1986.

Goodstein had a bipolar personality: he could be thoroughly charming or else display a terrifying anger, often intimidating enemies over the phone. For instance, Goodstein's personal war with Bill Madden of the New York *Daily News* was legendary in the business. Madden said, "I felt that Goodstein was all about promoting himself, that he was in this business strictly to get his name in the paper. He would actually say things like, "Make sure you use my name." Right there, my antennae went up. To me, Goodstein epitomized everything that was wrong about baseball. He was the stereotypical sleazy agent.

"We fought for years, and he would come up to me on the street and say, 'Why do you hate me?' And I'd say, 'Because you're basically a bullshit artist.'" Yet Goodstein's charm won over George Steinbrenner, which led to his greatest negotiating coup of all in 1987, getting Righetti a three-year, $10 million deal. Using as leverage a threat to take the left-hander to Japan, which Madden denounced as fiction, Goodstein outmaneuvered Steinbrenner into offering that third year, forcing the Yankee owner to bid against himself. When Steinbrenner realized he'd been beaten, he swore never to negotiate with Goodstein again. Yet the two remained friends after Righetti signed with the Giants as a free agent in 1991.

Strawberry was eager for this marriage with Goodstein, considering there were few, if any, offers for representation. And with Righetti's career winding down with the White Sox, Goodstein welcomed another big-name client into his life—only he didn't realize that serving as Darryl's agent meant becoming his guardian as well.

Suddenly, Goodstein found he was managing Darryl's already strained finances. With a $350,000 bill from the government, nearly $200,000 in fees due Gelfand's law firm in Los Angeles, and the crushing weight of Lisa Strawberry's $50,000-a-month support, Darryl was near financial collapse.

At one point during the summer, officers from the Sheriff's Department impounded two of Strawberry's sports cars, a result of Lisa's complaints of nonpayment. It wasn't long before Goodstein's entire law practice on Madison Avenue was devoted to keeping Strawberry afloat—financially and emotionally—long enough for him to return to baseball.

While Darryl was counting down the days of his suspension, Goodstein was choosing among three options. First, he could file a grievance against the Giants for releasing Darryl after they'd offered him arbitration. If Strawberry won, he would immediately return to the Giants. Second, Goodstein could lean on an old friendship with White Sox owner Jerry Reinsdorf and place Strawberry in Chicago as a designated hitter. Or else there was Steinbrenner and the Yankees.

That was the most intriguing possibility because it meant a chance for Strawberry to complete the circle of his life. "It's where I started, and it's where I wanted to go back to in the long run," he said. "I always said the fans in New York never got to see what I was really about, how well I could really perform. Part of that was my fault. Playing for the Yankees would show everyone that I'd changed my life."

There were ego motivations all around: Goodstein wanted to show he could still negotiate a megadeal with Steinbrenner and return to the ranks of big-name agents. Steinbrenner wanted to demonstrate that he, personally, would be the one who reformed the incorrigible Strawberry. And Yankee manager Buck Showalter had his own interest in Strawberry. One day at the stadium during batting practice, Showalter said, "I don't know what kind of trouble he's been in in the past, but if Darryl can still hit, I'd let him play for me."

Why not? From a pure baseball perspective, it looked like a worthy gamble. Surely, Steinbrenner wouldn't have to pay much for Strawberry, and most of the money could be tied into incentives. One drug slipup and Strawberry could be made to disappear. And if Strawberry could stay clean . . . well, there was the matter of a 296-foot porch in right field, which was so tailored to Strawberry's massive uppercut that it wasn't impossible to think of him hitting twenty-five home runs in half a season.

The Yankees had left-handed power in their 1995 lineup, but certainly no one could match Darryl—or at least the old Darryl—for home-run potential. Paul O'Neill was a fine line-drive hitter but not a forty-homer threat. And Don Mattingly, troubled by a weakened back, wasn't scaring pitchers anymore, not as he used to in the mid-eighties.

But as much as Strawberry's presence made sense to some, the image of him in pinstripes was too much for many Yankee loyalists. That Darryl be allowed to grace the same uniform worn by Ruth, Gehrig, DiMaggio, and Mantle . . . well, a pariah like Jim Bouton couldn't help but smirk. Expelled from the Yankee community ever since he authored *Ball Four* in 1970—and still banned from Old Timers' Games to this day—Bouton said, "I guess I would've had an easier time coming back to the Yankees if I'd done drugs or pleaded guilty to tax evasion."

Interestingly, though, one of Strawberry's most vocal sympathizers was Pete Rose, who had every right to resent Darryl's light sentence. After all, Rose had done five and a half months for tax evasion, even though he paid back every penny, including fines and interest, a week before his sentencing. But Rose asked, "How is Darryl Strawberry going to jail ever going to change what happened to me? Jail was such a horrible experience, I wouldn't wish it on my worst enemy. That's how humiliating it was. Mike Schmidt kept asking me when I was doing time, 'When can I come see you?' I told him, 'Mike, I don't want you to see me like this.' I didn't even want to see my family. If Darryl learned his lesson without having to go to jail, God bless him. Tell him I wish him good luck."

It wasn't long before Strawberry heard Rose's comments and made a special appearance on Rose's radio show:

"He was one of the few guys out there who knew what my situation was like. Pete understood," Strawberry said. "Everyone was having so much fun, talking behind my back, that I made up my mind that once I got back to baseball, I wasn't gonna talk anymore. Just go about my business and show everyone they were wrong."

Clearly, Darryl needed a stage. Only where? The Giants wished Darryl good luck . . . but not in San Francisco. They were preparing to fight any grievance Goodstein filed. And while Reinsdorf listened politely while Goodstein described how much damage Strawberry could do in tandem with Frank Thomas, it was clear the White Sox weren't going to pay much more than the major-league minimum—barely above $100,000.

It was George who awaited Darryl. There had been only one path all along, and it led directly to the Bronx.

FOR SIX HOURS, at 35,000 feet, Strawberry felt free—flying first-class, far away from the IRS, getting closer and closer to Steinbrenner. On June 23, at 5:48 P.M., on the moment American Airlines flight 928 landed at Tampa Airport, Darryl began his new life with the Yankees. He looked out the window of the 727 and saw exactly what that meant: four Tampa police cars, Hillsborough County sheriffs, and Yankee security personnel waiting on the runway.

Strawberry paused a moment, his eyebrows flexing slightly. He'd planned to meet Dwight Gooden at the arrival gate, but Darryl never made it that far. He was whisked away by a pack of thick-muscled men in dark suits and with walkie-talkies. Strawberry was also meaning to have dinner with the Goodens in St. Petersburg, but that plan was obliterated, too. This time, it was the Feds, who decided Strawberry's house arrest— shifted to Florida while he played himself into shape—would confine him to the Bay Harbor Inn on Tampa's outskirts.

That meant for the next six days, Darryl was only allowed to hit batting-practice fastballs and eat room-service dinner. He could accept no phone calls unless they were first screened by an operator, and there were be no unannounced visitors to his room. It was Strawberry's welcome to King George's fiefdom.

"I'm taking a gamble on this young man, not as a ballplayer but on his life," Steinbrenner said. The introduction spoke of mistrust, of how little the Yankees were leaving to Strawberry's own personal choice. As a Yankee, he would be living in a tightly controlled environment, with little access to the public or media. Darryl had planned on residing at the Holiday Inn in Secaucus, New Jersey, once he joined the Yankees, but federal authorities stipulated that when the Yankees were home, Strawberry would have to live in Westchester County, where he was found guilty of tax evasion. Steinbrenner further alluded to "several plans" the Yankees had for Darryl's off-field life, which were to be monitored by their security chief, Jack Lawn, a former Drug Enforcement Agency chief, and, later, by James Williams, another former DEA head.

Darryl spoke with some passion about wanting to "get away from controversies from now on." The press nodded politely, copied the words into their notebooks, and wondered how soon they could escape the sun. Of course, everyone had heard similar pronouncements from Strawberry over the years—in fact, the words nearly sounded rehearsed. All that mattered was the answer to two questions: could Darryl still hit, and could he stay clean?

Strawberry knew what the doubters were thinking. "I've made a lot of mistakes in my life, but I never hurt anyone except myself. But I know I can still play baseball, and I'm very thankful to the Yankees and Mr. Steinbrenner that I've been given a chance to do that. I want to prove to everyone that I'm not that bad of a guy, that I'm worth this chance. So after today, I'm not going to be doing much talking. I kind of want to take care of myself and stay away from controversies for a change."

Darryl sounded stiff and uncomfortable with Steinbrenner standing right next to him. That was understandable.

At least Strawberry looked good wearing a dark-blue Yankee jersey, the number twenty-six barely housing his Nautilus-honed muscles. Strawberry put on a pleasing twenty-minute show on that first day at Yankee camp, taking 120 swings in the cage, his bat speed still looking impressive.

Still, Steinbrenner admitted, "I have no idea if Darryl can help us. It's been two years since he really played." Incredibly, the Yankees never scouted Strawberry while he was working out with the Palm Springs Suns, an independent team, and no one consulted Buck Showalter as to how to fit Strawberry into the Yankee system.

What Steinbrenner was doing was gambling—both on Strawberry's immediate resurrection and the public's acceptance. But not everyone was ready to embrace Darryl. In fact, the protest came from as high up as the White House, where Lee Brown—President Clinton's drug czar—said allowing Darryl to return to baseball "was sending the wrong message to our kids."

Strawberry and Goodstein were stunned at Brown's comments.

"What did I ever do to him?" Darryl said. And Goodstein added, "This would be a perfect chance to use Darryl as a role model for second chances—that it is possible to rehabilitate yourself. I don't know who Brown is trying to win points with, but his position is idiotic."

Unfortunately for Strawberry, though, Steinbrenner was so startled by Brown's comment, one aide said, "George started to look for an out clause that very first day." Strawberry might have thought he'd cleared the final hurdle in his return to the big leagues, but he didn't realize his new employers weren't the Mets, and Frank Cashen wasn't in charge. Darryl was a Yankee now, and one Met executive said, "The poor S.O.B. doesn't know what he just got himself into."

9

TWELVE STEPS
FROM HELL

THE SUN HAD nearly surrendered to the night, which made it difficult for Dwight Gooden and his friends to see exactly whose car it was that had just pulled onto Tampa's Thirtieth Street Southeast. Instinctively, Gooden took a step back, and his three friends—a cousin and two acquaintances from Tampa—formed a protective circle around him. The trio was unofficially designated as Doc's bodyguards until the police determined who it was that had threatened the life of his sister, Betty Jones, the mother of Gary Sheffield.

Someone had telephoned Betty Jones and told her a bullet was waiting for her. Gooden had no doubt the lunatic was after Sheffield, and since his nephew lived only two houses away, Doc thought it would be safer if he were surrounded by muscle. This was December of 1994, and Gooden had virtually disappeared from the baseball community. As far as anyone in the commissioner's office was concerned, Gooden, still wrestling with drug addiction, was a nonentity, suspended for the entire '95 season. That's what made Doc so suspicious about the two strangers now approaching him: who would bother to visit him at this point in his life? He was down, almost out, and not really in the mood for visitors.

"Who's that? Get the fuck outta here," Gooden said menacingly. His bodyguards had fanned out across the street and were in near attack formation. Unless Doc heard a satisfactory answer within seconds, his friends would launch a preemptory strike.

The reporter from New York didn't understand the threat before him. He'd known Gooden for years and had dropped into town to see him, but he hadn't heard about the threat on Betty Jones's life and had no idea why Gooden seemed so nervous. He sure didn't know who the three angry thugs walking straight for him were.

"Doc, it's me," the newsman said nervously. He had come for an interview, not a street fight.

Gooden's voice softened immediately. "Fuck, man, why didn't you say it was you?" he asked with a laugh. Turning to his friends, Doc said, "It's okay, I know him."

"You ought to be more careful around here. You almost got your ass kicked, cuz."

The reporter explained that he'd been having trouble finding Gooden's house and had enlisted the help of another St. Pete resident who had his own connections in the baseball world: Ray Negron, a thirty-nine-year-old agent. The reporter introduced Gooden to Negron. Doc nodded hello, then tilted his head in the direction of his friends and said cryptically, "These guys are with me."

It was clear the introductions wouldn't go any further, and maybe it was better that way. The newsman was dis-

turbed by what he heard and saw that day. Even in ex-
changing pleasantries, Gooden had a hostile edge that he
had never exhibited in all his years at Shea. There was the
smell of alcohol in the air, too, although it was impossible
to tell who among Doc's party was actually drinking. But
that street-tough side of Gooden, even the way his Mercedes
was appointed, with oversized chrome rims, suggested ag-
gression.

Doc had always been the kindest of the superstar Mets, particularly when it came to dealing with the press. He never said
no to anyone, and this had begun in 1984, his rookie year,
when P.R. director Jay Horwitz said, "We had a week when
seven different magazines wanted to put Dwight on the
cover—and I said yes to all of them. Dwight went along with
it. It was a terrible mistake on my part."

Gooden declined to be interviewed at this moment, telling
the newsman, "Now's not a good time." At least Gooden had
learned to say no, and there was something in the tone of his
voice that suggested any argument from the newsman would
be useless, maybe even met with hostility. Actually, Doc
seemed more interested in the baseball man, Negron. They
spent a few minutes talking, and Gooden learned that Negron
was partners with a New York lawyer named Bill Goodstein
and also had ties to Japanese baseball. Also intriguing to
Gooden was that Negron acted as a direct liaison in the
United States for the Tokyo Giants.

Naturally, Negron had heard all about Gooden's troubles in
recent months, but he never was presumptuous enough to
present himself at Doc's door. Gooden was still being represented by Jim Neader, a St. Petersburg neighbor who had
been Doc's front man since his rookie year. To pursue Gooden
in any way would have been unethical to Negron, yet he

sensed he'd made a friend in Gooden, even in the few minutes they chatted.

Maybe it wasn't so surprising that two days later when Negron answered a knock on his door, there was Gooden, holding his young daughter in his arms. "You got a minute to talk?" Doc asked. Negron asked his guest to step into the house, and the two men began to exchange ideas on baseball, Japan, and, of greatest interest to Gooden, addiction.

"There was something Ray said to me that first time that made me think he understood what drugs can do to someone. I got the feeling he might've had a firsthand experience," Gooden said. "A lot of people on the outside think they know what they're talking about, especially the ones who were always putting me down. But it's not so easy unless you've been there. I wanted to find out what Ray really knew."

It turned out Gooden's intuition about Negron was correct. In fact, the agent's history was far more colorful than Gooden could ever have known. Of Puerto Rican descent, Negron grew up in Queens, and when he was twenty-two suspected a younger brother was involved with cocaine. It started when Negron saw the brother stealing money out of his mother's purse, although it wasn't until his mother started complaining about the missing money that Negron began to understand the clues.

"My mother was a schoolteacher, my father was an orderly at a hospital. Obviously, we didn't come from a lot of money," Negron said. "So the money was a big deal when it was gone. I had heard rumors about my brother, and one day I finally asked him to his face, 'Are you using cocaine?'

"He started crying right in front of me and asked me to help him. He said he was trying to get off the stuff and that he needed money to get some counseling—without my parents knowing about it. I gave him a couple of bucks, and that's what kept the cycle going. I realize now I'd become an enabler."

Over the course of several years, Negron's brother perpetually milked him for money, the demands easing or increasing depending on how deep the addiction ran at a particular time. The dependency might have gone on forever had it not been for a 2 A.M. phone call Negron got from his brother from somewhere in east Brooklyn eight years earlier.

"He told me some dealers were going to kill him if he didn't come up with two hundred dollars, and could I come right away?" Negron recalled. "I drove like crazy to get there and showed up, like an idiot. I thought I was helping my brother. I got to the place he told me he was, walked into a hallway of some dark building—I was scared out of my mind—and I felt a gun to my head. Some guy said, 'Just give me the fucking money.' I gave him the two hundred dollars, turned around, and went home, thanking God I didn't get shot. My brother denies it to this day, but I think he set me up, just for the cash."

When he finished telling this story, Negron said to Gooden, "Listen, Dwight, I know you need help. There's places around here you can go. I can reach out to a few people." Negron knew that addiction could steal a life in more ways than just drugs. Having grown up less than a mile from Belmont Park, he saw how the lure of gambling could be just as powerful as coke or crack. "One friend of mine lost all his savings in that place in the course of a few months, steadily went through everything he ever had. It was awful to watch," Negron said. "His whole life was about catching up . . . just one more payoff . . . just one more winner. He was only fooling himself because it never ends unless you admit you're sick."

Negron offered Gooden help at a twelve-step program in St. Petersburg. Gooden took the offer seriously, knowing he had nothing to lose. "I was still in denial at that point, and nothing had seemed to help, so I thought, yeah, why not try those twelve-step programs," Gooden said. "I was still thinking in the back of my mind that I could come back to baseball some-time in ninety-five, even though I had a year suspension. But before I could even think about getting the commissioner to think of it, I wanted to get clean again. I had to get clean."

Gooden said yes, and his professional relationship with Ne-gron began. Doc also asked Negron for a favor: even though he was still linked with Neader, would Negron explore the possibility of Doc's going to Japan in '95? Negron, who had sent a respectable number of players to the Far East, including Jesse Barfield, Lloyd Moseby, and Henry Cotto, told Gooden he would do his best but the odds were overwhelmingly against Doc. Not only was his surgically repaired arm a risk in the eyes of the Japanese—not to mention losing records in 1992, '93, and '94—but Gooden's history with drugs would almost certainly doom him, too. An executive of the Tokyo Giants said, "As big a name as Dwight Gooden once had in the United States, our standards for American players are ex-tremely high. They must be model citizens as long as they are guests in our country. We take no risks."

Gooden, of course, didn't care. For him, nothing was worse than sitting in St. Petersburg every day, not knowing when and if he could return to baseball. All Gooden knew was that his ca-reer with the Mets was over. "I really didn't want to go back there anymore, not the way we left things," Doc said. "But after that, I had no idea what I wanted or where I was going."

His first stop was the twelve-step meeting in downtown St. Petersburg. Gooden and Negron arrived together because it was important for Gooden to understand the chapter's chemistry. Unlike the AA meetings Gooden had attended in New York, the St. Pete support group wasn't filled with middle-class sports fans. Gooden was shocked to see street people, many of them hard-core junkies, just trying to get through another day. "They couldn't care less who I was, or what I'd been doing with my life, or the circumstances of me getting there," Gooden said. "That was my first real positive feeling I had about recovery in a long, long time. I walked in there and said, 'Maybe this time it's going to work.' "

That reaction was in sharp contrast to the denial Gooden exhibited in 1987, when he was horrified by the addicts he met in Smithers. But Doc's fall from grace had been steep. Vincent Kenyon said, "The most important part of Dwight's recovery was that he was no longer ashamed of himself. He stopped feeling like he had to hide his illness."

Gooden may have had a positive intuition about the place, but the group's leader, Ron Dock, was ready to reject the pitcher the moment he saw him. "I remember that first day Dwight walked in. I didn't say a word to him, I just watched. I've been around addicts long enough to know that Dwight was totally bankrupt, both morally and spiritually, when he came to us. He sat in the corner, not saying a word, looking like he was desperate for help. I'm telling you, man, the dude was bankrupt in every aspect."

Gooden was indeed too shy to speak to the group in his first day. He sat in the corner, just as Dock described it, and listened. When Dock's turn to speak came, he revealed a powerful story of addiction—and recovery. In fact, the details of Dock's addiction moved Gooden so deeply he asked the leader to be his personal sponsor.

Dock was a forty-five-year-old Bronx native, a former marine who had served in Vietnam. He stood 6-0 and, at little more than 160 pounds, was a portrait of lean-muscle mass. Dock had a blunt, direct style, and he had no trouble asking Gooden, "How bad do you want to stay clean?"

"Real bad," Gooden said.

"Well, if you do, then just come back here tomorrow," Dock said. "That's it. You're talking too much as it is. The only thing you can do to prove to me you're serious is show up again."

Dock turned around and walked away, unsure if Gooden would return and not really interested. As he put it, "I've seen so many addicts come and go, they talk a good game, until it's really time to surrender to the disease. That's when they decide to come back to me. It was up to Dwight to decide if he wanted to be clean and not just say so."

Gooden thought about the years and years of addiction and how tired he was of the endless cycle: drinking, using, the brief but exhilarating high, the crash, and then, always, the guilt. Doc knew that in all the years since he'd started his romance with the drug—all the parties he went to, all the laughter he thought he was enjoying, all the times his heart was beating fast and his mind seemed to be racing in hyperspace—he was never happier than when he was pitching well and staying sober.

If only every day could be like it was in 1986, when the world was his, when he and Darryl were two buddies playing for the best team in the major leagues. That was long before his life became a currency of white lies, all used to cover his addiction. Doc wondered if Narcotics Anonymous was the true path to finding a more peaceful past. Could it hurt to try? "The doctors at Smithers and Betty Ford all offered me the same advice about life in the real world. They said, 'Make sure you get help on the outside; get help, join a support group. Don't try to do this all by yourself.' " Well, here it was, in the form of a crazy, skinny marine who didn't care that Dwight Gooden was the youngest Cy Young Award winner in the history of the major leagues or that he had been New York's most popular athlete in the eighties.

In fact, no one really cared who Gooden was. This sure wasn't New York, where being a celebrity meant making the most money, knowing the most famous people, winning the most games . . . and, then, getting as high as possible. Gooden decided, "I can live this lifestyle. At least I can try." He returned the next day to Ron Dock's meeting.

DOCK STOOD BEFORE his group and prepared to share his story. Many had heard it before, some had not. No matter. It was the sharing that bonded the addicts, a lesson that Gooden would soon learn. In fact, many of the anecdotes addicts told were surprisingly similar—and the sooner other addicts came to that revelation, the sooner they understood they weren't alone with their disease.

Yet, even by NA standards, Dock had an unusually powerful history with drugs, which started in 1968 in the jungles of Southeast Asia. "I went to Evander Childs High School in the Bronx, and I was going nowhere in my life. I was boxing in the PAL, running a little track, but I had no real goals," he said. "I didn't know anything about the marines or Vietnam until one of my best friends, an older guy, a Puerto Rican, came home one day in his dress blues. And, man, that wiped me off the map. He looked so tough, so sharp. I was so bored with my life at the time, I decided I had to join up.

"Funny thing was, I didn't know the first thing about racism until I got into the Corps. The sergeants started on me right away, telling me, 'Hey, boy, we're gonna kill you when we get you to Nam. You gonna die, you know that?' Shit, I thought these guys were supposed to be on my side. Was I scared? You better believe it. I was only seventeen when I went over, got into my first firefight within two weeks.

"It was three in the afternoon, and I was part of a seven-man patrol getting ready to set up an ambush when we got caught in an L-shaped ambush ourselves. The VC started with mortars, then with AK-47 fire, and right away we were pinned down in the rice paddies. We lost one marine, and another was about two minutes away from dying when we called in for an artillery strike. Luckily, the VC broke off contact with us.

"Well, it happened so fast, I never realized that during the firefight, I had urinated and defecated on myself. I was screaming, completely crazy; I'd gone into shock. I knew Vietnam was not for me, but there I was, stuck in the worst place in the world. My buddy in the dress blues didn't tell me what being a marine was really about—constant fear. And man, I was about over the edge. My sergeant gave me a little weed, some Jim Beam, and I passed out. And that's how it started."

From that point on, Dock became reliant on drugs to get himself through Vietnam. The marines suffered a casualty rate of over 75 percent during the conflict, and everywhere Dock looked someone was either dying or close to dying. So when the urge to cry or run came over Dock, he got high, and soon the anxiety just went away. Dock found opium to be especially comforting whenever he had to go on the most dangerous of assignments, night patrol; the consolation was that he found so many marines doing it as well. "Put it this way," he said.

"Whenever we killed a VC, the first thing we did was check his pockets for opium."

Within six months, Dock learned to welcome fear because it gave him an excuse to get high. In fact, fear became the addiction as much as the opium itself, and he routinely would volunteer for night patrol. Dock was only half surprised to discover one night, during an especially fierce firefight, that he developed an erection while firing his M-16 rifle.

"It was total power for me over my fears. Here I was, an eighteen-year-old black kid with a rifle, with permission to kill people. I loved it. In fact, I was addicted to it," Dock said. He eventually came home, and the disease followed. Dock was assigned to the marine base in Quantico, and it was his job to teach young lieutenants the basics of jungle warfare. He recalled, "I was still so crazy, I rebelled. I said, 'Fuck that, I ain't teaching no one nothing.' " Dock briefly took over the Veterans Administration Hospital, holding several doctors hostage in the emergency room. Although the situation was quickly defused, Dock's career as a marine was over. He was dishonorably discharged and sent back to the Bronx.

For more than twenty years, Dock's life was a blur of petty crimes, arrests, and, always, drugs. Jail didn't help Dock get sober and hospitals and psychiatry were failures as well. A brief attempt at marriage was no match for his love of drugs, and he was divorced within months. Then, one day it came to Dock as an epiphany: living in the streets of St. Petersburg, eating from garbage bins, and weighing 142 pounds, he decided, "I was going to die, maybe that day."

He approached a police officer and said, "Please, take me to a treatment center." And from that day on, it got better. It had been over three years since Dock had become sober, and one of the first lessons he taught Gooden was "You're never going to beat this thing altogether. It will be with you the rest of your life."

With his introduction to the twelve steps, Gooden learned that his recovery came before anything in his life, including his wife, Monica, his children, his parents, even baseball. Without recovery, none of his other passions would be there for him. Gooden had plenty of long-range plans on his mind: return to baseball, win the Comeback Player of the Year Award, get back to the World Series, and, mostly, reestablish his name in the baseball world. That's what ate at Gooden most of all: "The way I left the game. I don't want people twenty years from now to say, 'Dwight Gooden had a great career, but he threw it away.' I want them to say, 'Dwight Gooden had a great career because he beat his problem.' I sure don't want my kids to think of their father as some junkie who couldn't handle success."

Dock listened to Gooden's hopes and aspirations, then cut him short. "If you really want to impress me," the counselor said, "then don't think about anything except tomorrow. Your goal from now on is to stay clean for the next twenty-four hours."

IN A PERFECT world, Dwight Gooden's involvement with the twelve-step program would have wiped away not only his abuse of cocaine but the urge for it as well. If only there were a magic pill, Gooden thought, that could be ingested and used to defeat the devil. But Gooden had learned long ago there was no escaping the moments of weakness, even with the strong support he was getting from Ron Dock. It was Dock who reemphasized an old twelve-step message: in order to stay sober, Gooden would have to change the people and places of his addictive world. It was sound advice—Gooden knew that. Only it was sometimes easier said than done.

On March 19, 1995, Gooden was coming home from a night out in Tampa. The digital clock in his BMW said 4:00 A.M., and with Interstate 275 all but deserted, a feeling of déjà vu washed over Gooden. He pushed the car over one hundred miles per hour just because he'd done it so many times before and had never been caught. Gooden knew it was a foolish driving decision, one made even more reckless because he'd just taken a long pull on a bottle of Red Dog beer, a complete and indefensible mistake for any recovering addict.

If there are troubling areas in Gooden's recovery, they are found in the events of this night. He was clocked by the Florida Highway Patrol at 117 miles per hour and, after a brief pursuit, was pulled over by two troopers. Recognizing Gooden and fully aware of his past difficulties with police, the troopers asked if they could search the car.

"Yes, sir, go right ahead," Gooden said politely, in sharp contrast to the tone he'd used in the fight with Tampa police eight years earlier. The police found the half-empty bottle of Red Dog and another unopened bottle. They also found a .9mm pistol, which, because it was unloaded and in the glove compartment, was not in violation of any Florida law. But because there was beer on Gooden's breath, the officers asked him to step out of the car.

According to Lieutenant Harold Frear of the FHP, the two troopers conducted a thorough field sobriety test and were satisfied that Gooden was not impaired by the beer, or under the influence of any drugs. "If there was any doubt at all, Mr. Gooden would have been arrested on the spot," Lieutenant Frear said. "The officers said he was fine and, in fact, conducted himself in a nonthreatening manner. He was issued a ticket and was sent on his way without any further problems."

Indeed, Gooden passed all his drug tests in the subsequent week, so it was evident that he wasn't high at the time he was speeding. But Negron and attorney Bill Goodstein, whom Gooden had officially designated as his agents on April 1, were shocked that Gooden never told them of the incident. It was only after the *St. Petersburg Times* ran the story on April 25 that Goodstein and Negron learned about it. Gooden dismissed the matter as "nothing really important" and left his co-agents with the unpleasant chore of spin control. For some reason, Gooden told the press he'd been coming home from a night out with friends, all of whom had attended a basketball game at the University of South Florida.

But the game was played on March 17, and the date on the speeding ticket was March 19. As for the beer on his breath, Gooden explained he'd just dropped off his cousin Chris in Tampa after he and some other friends had been eating at a Miami Subs shop. Gooden said he remained in the car while Chris—the son of his sister Betty—went inside. Gooden asked for a gyro and a Diet Coke but only got the gyro. "We were already on the way when I realized I had nothing to drink," Gooden said, which is why he took a pull of Chris's Red Dog when the sandwich became lodged in his throat.

Gooden took responsibility for the series of mistakes, saying, "I should've known better than to be driving that fast, and there's no excuse for drinking a beer. But it wasn't mine." The newspapers had a wonderful time with the story, and major-league baseball promised to investigate whether Gooden had further violated his aftercare program.

Because Gooden was not arrested, or even charged with drunken driving—and because his subsequent tests showed no traces of cocaine—the matter soon died. But Gooden was harshly lectured by Goodstein, who said, "I have a reputation to uphold. I'm a lifelong Democrat, I'm a Kennedy man—I helped Robert Kennedy in his New York presidential campaign in nineteen sixty-eight. I don't need any more problems from you. The next time there's trouble like this, I'm gone."

Gooden gave Goodstein his word, and that day the lawyer told reporters, "As long as I'm representing Dwight Gooden, there will be no further incidents of this kind. I can guarantee it." Yet neither Negron nor Goodstein ever learned what actually happened that night, and neither agent ever chose to push Gooden for an answer.

The reason Goodstein so desperately needed Gooden's co-operation was simple: he was beginning to mount a campaign to have Doc reinstated sometime in 1995. Although Doc's suspension was supposed to last the entire season, Goodstein was planning to take advantage of the personal friendship he enjoyed with one of baseball's most powerful owners, the White Sox's Jerry Reinsdorf. Not only was Reinsdorf a member of baseball's executive council, but he also had the ear of Acting Commissioner Bud Selig. If Reinsdorf could be convinced that Gooden was clean—and that his return would not embarrass the owners—then perhaps Selig could be indirectly influenced, too. Ultimately, it was Selig who would determine Gooden's fate, although it would be many months before Doc would be able to make a strong case for himself.

First, Selig was busy trying to heal baseball's wounds, as the sport was just ending the longest and most damaging strike in its history. And Gooden set himself back at least two months as a result of his speeding incident. What Gooden needed, more than anything else, was several months of invisibility—a nonstop series of negative drug tests and plenty of meetings.

One other factor was weighing heavily on Gooden's future as well: he needed Darryl Strawberry to stay clean, now that he'd avoided jail and was planning to return to baseball sometime that summer. If Strawberry had another relapse, no owner in baseball would dare take a chance on Gooden.

Who hadn't read the *Sports Illustrated* article that ran in late February 1995 in which Gooden and Strawberry both revealed the depth of the Mets' drug use in the eighties? The club was profoundly embarrassed by their former players' revelations and severed relations with them. P.R. director Horwitz, who considered himself one of Dwight's closest friends even after he was suspended, said it would take "a long, long time" before he would ever call Gooden again. Not that Gooden minded. He said, "I read the article and everything in it was accurate. If the Mets can't accept that they had some wild players, then it's their problem, not mine."

In the eighties, when Gooden and Strawberry were at the peak of their athletic abilities, it didn't matter who they offended. But the nineties brought each player closer to the vicious currency of baseball politics, where decisions are often made on personal likes and dislikes. People needed to be reminded that Dwight Gooden was once New York's most popular player, not just its most dominant. Starting in April, Negron and Goodstein informally divided the responsibility of handling their two clients. Goodstein would navigate through Strawberry's legal problems and find Darryl a job later that summer, and Negron, who lived only four miles from Gooden in St. Petersburg, would oversee his day-to-day recovery.

One of Negron's decisions was to introduce Gooden to a longtime friend, Vincent Kenyon, a former Wall Street broker whose own career was sabotaged by cocaine in 1991. Battling addiction for almost three years, Kenyon had left New York and divided his time between Atlanta, where his parents lived, and St. Petersburg. Kenyon and Gooden became instant friends, and, with the support he was getting from Ron Dock, it appeared Gooden was finally on the path to recovery.

One of the reasons Gooden and Kenyon bonded so perfectly was that the businessman was so blunt in admitting he still craved drugs—not just cocaine but crack, too. "I told Dwight, 'If you think of cocaine as a mellow high, like slowly climbing stairs, then using crack is like getting on an express elevator all the way to the top,'" Kenyon said. "It's a very powerful high, and in many people, it creates paranoia. You think everyone is out to get you, you think everyone is an undercover cop. You cannot defeat crack unless you get help. If you're in denial, it will kill you."

Gooden and Kenyon would drive through the old neighborhoods in Tampa, and Doc would point out where he used to buy drugs. "Doc told me about one time when he was driving around everywhere, going crazy because he couldn't find anyone to sell to him, and so he just took his car out on the highway, pushing it as fast as he could," Kenyon said. "He was very, very down about the control the drugs had over him, about the way it was affecting his personality, how everything irritated him, how he was taking it out on Monica at home." Gooden never struck his wife, but his anger was intimidating nonetheless: he could go days without speaking to his wife or Negron if he felt he'd been wronged. Unlike Darryl, whose anger flashed and then evaporated, Gooden simmered.

The turning point in Gooden's recovery, at least in Kenyon's mind, came right after Father's Day, when Doc addressed the other addicts at NA. According to Kenyon, Gooden stood before the group and said, "My father has never been much of a talker, he never really said a lot to me in all the years that I was growing up. Well, yesterday, I put my arms around my dad and said, 'Happy Father's Day, Dad. I love you.' And my dad said, 'I love you very much, Dwight.' "

Gooden was so moved by the exchange, he started crying into his father's shoulder. And in telling the story again, Gooden broke down again. "That's how I decided, 'He's going to make it,' " Kenyon said. "I felt that he was getting in touch with things inside of him that he'd been out of touch with before."

While Gooden was trying to heal from within, he was also determined to rehabilitate his arm. It had been nearly a year since he last pitched for the Mets, and while the rest may have refreshed the muscles in his rotator cuff, there would come a point where Gooden's skills would begin to atrophy. He hired Larry Mayol, a trainer with the Mets in the early eighties, to develop an exercise and conditioning regimen, and along with Negron and a few local college kids, he began throwing every other day at Eckerd College. It was an odd sight, a former major leaguer dressed in torn-up shorts and a T-shirt, pitching off an abandoned mound to his agent. But Gooden was determined to be ready if and when he got an early reprieve from major-league baseball.

"And who knows, what if some scout happens to be in the area and comes by to see me throw?" Gooden asked. "I want them to know that I'm serious about getting back to where I used to be."

Negron kept encouraging Gooden, no matter how difficult it might have been to be on the field every Monday-Wednesday-Friday at 8 A.M. That's because as his friend, Negron knew "it was very, very important for Dwight to have a goal in his life—

getting back in ninety-five—and also having some structure. If he had to be getting out of bed so early every day, it was less likely that he'd be out late the previous night. The workouts were as therapeutic as anything else in his life."

Gooden was so seduced by his return to baseball—even in the scaled-down surroundings of a college field—that he joined a local amateur league. One of his workout buddies was a former Double-A pitcher named Doug Kemp, who had become friends with Negron. Like many minor leaguers whose careers end short of a big-league contract, Kemp couldn't just turn away from baseball. Hence, he joined St. Petersburg's Stan Musial League, a league for anyone eighteen and up. Mostly, the players were college kids home for the summer or, like Kemp, former Class A and Double-A stars. Kemp asked Gooden if he was interested in playing for his team, the Red Tide, and Gooden found the idea appealing.

"I mean, I wasn't about to go on the mound and pitch, that wouldn't do anyone any good, but I sort of liked the idea of getting a few at-bats again," Gooden said. "More than anything else, it was the idea of putting on a uniform, being part of a team again. I needed to compete."

Negron obviously was terrified. "What if Doc gets hurt?" he asked. Indeed, there was no guarantee that an overzealous amateur wouldn't hit Gooden in the head or the shoulder with an errant fastball, and then what? Negron tried to persuade Gooden that his steady workouts were all the preparation he needed for a comeback, but he also knew there was no arguing with Doc. His mind was cemented to the idea of playing ball.

Gooden's first game was against a team called the Hurricanes, and while they didn't feel any embarrassment gawking at Gooden, his teammates were unsure how to act. "Everyone wanted to ask for an autograph or just make small talk with him. After all, he was Dwight Gooden," Kemp said. "But at the same time, no one wanted to turn the dugout into a circus. We were still a team."

Gooden did his part by acting naturally, encouraging his teammates when they were at bat, treating the game as seriously as any nine innings he ever played at Shea. Gooden originally wanted to play first base, but Negron insisted this was a needless risk, especially with the possibility of a line drive or a collision in the base path. Finally, it was decided that Gooden would play left field, where it was safer.

Gooden had no trouble hitting amateur pitchers, easily topping .300. Swinging the bat was always Gooden's passion anyway, and he'd rattled off to his teammates the list of major-league pitchers he'd taken deep. "John Smoltz was my favorite," Gooden said of the Braves' star right-hander. "He tried to throw a fastball by me, and I crushed it. One of the longest home runs I ever hit."

Maybe it was no surprise when, in the ninth inning against the Hurricanes, with the Red Tide leading 1–0, Gooden whispered to Kemp in the dugout, "I'm gonna put this game out of reach." Doc stepped to the plate, and the very first pitch he saw was a high fastball. He swung, the arc as loose and long-limbed as his windup on the mound, and the ball connected with the sweet spot on the bat's barrel. No one had to study the parabola that ball was creating; the sound was proof enough that Gooden was good to his word. As he circled the bases, his smile was as wide and genuine as any he had worn that summer.

"What I really liked about playing for that team was they made me feel like one of them and not like I was some sort of celebrity," Gooden said. "It could've been uncomfortable, but they went out of their way to make it seem as normal as possible. Even guys on the other teams tried not to be weird about it, and that even went for the umpires. Everyone was very cool."

Gooden was so much a part of the Red Tide that, in the final weeks of the season, he was in the middle of a bench-clearing brawl. The play began with a runner on second rounding third after a base hit to center field, who then exploded when he crashed into the catcher at the plate. "You could just tell it was going to happen, even before it did," Kemp said. Within moments, some thirty players were in one another's faces, and there was Gooden, trying to separate them. "The funny thing was, Doc's presence on the field helped quiet things down," Kemp said. "As soon as everyone realized he was serious about it, risking injury to himself, we sort of said, 'Whoa, we better stop.' Pretty soon, everyone started talking to him, just shootin' the breeze. Even the umpires dug him."

THE PHONE CALL was made in panic, which isn't unusual when the source of the crisis is drugs. It was Negron who was calling Gooden, and the news was all bad: Vincent Kenyon had suffered a relapse somewhere in downtown St. Pete and had telephoned Negron claiming he had been taken hostage by drug dealers.

Negron was instantly suspicious, since he'd heard that story so many times in his own past. No doubt Kenyon had run out of money during a crack binge and was creating a false emergency to feed his habit. A part of Negron just wanted to hang up the phone because even after this crisis was handled, he knew somewhere, sometime, there would be another. It was impossible not to be weary of the battle. But what choice did Negron have except to rescue his friend one more time?

He could very easily have left Gooden out of it, but Negron made a point of calling him. For one thing, he and Kenyon were friends, and they had made a vow to each other to be there in case either one fell. But Negron also wanted Gooden to see, up close and in the flesh, what a crack addict looked like after his body was overloaded with the drug.

Kenyon had gone down without any warning three days earlier. He'd just taken a group of investors to the airport after they appeared to have agreed on a sports marketing deal. Kenyon still had strong business instincts and, when he was clean, could still network effectively. One of Kenyon's cocaine triggers, however, was money—or, more precisely, the promise of it.

"For some reason, the idea of coming into a big paycheck becomes more than I can handle psychologically," Kenyon would say later. "We had a plan that could work, and the urge just hit me after I dropped my partners off." Kenyon took his rented car to the southeast section of St. Pete and bought a hit of crack. Three days later he was calling Negron for help, already having lost all his money and even the car. In fact, Kenyon was so bankrupt the dealers had to loan him twenty-five cents for the phone call.

Yes, Gooden told Negron, he would be glad to help. He'd been worried about Kenyon for the three days he'd been missing, although, Doc said, "I had a feeling he'd gone down. I just had a sense something bad had happened to him." Gooden put the phone down, waited a moment, then called Ron Dock. He told his sponsor about Kenyon, and while Dock was, of course, concerned about a fallen addict, he was also worried about Gooden's own psychological state. Did he really need to be reminded of what a crack addict looks like? Did Gooden need any more exposure to the world of drugs than he'd already had?

Those were legitimate questions but ones to be wrestled with another day. Kenyon's safety came first. Negron rushed to Gooden's house, and then they picked up Dock. They decided it would be wiser to drive Negron's badly worn and beaten 1982 Subaru, which Negron kept as a reminder of the days when he was broke. Besides, an old car would look less conspicuous in the neighborhood they were about to travel into. And there was no doubt where Kenyon was: on Thirty-fourth Street, in the dangerous southeast section of town.

Before getting into the car, Gooden had taken five hundred dollars out of his wallet just to make sure Kenyon could be extracted from this mess. Gooden figured the situation would be bad, and he was right. When they pulled the car into an alley, the three men saw Kenyon sitting in a pile of trash. Standing over him were three muscular, dangerous-looking youths. Negron and Dock told Gooden, "Stay in the car, let us handle this." If the confrontation raged out of control, they wanted Gooden to be spared. At least he had a future to protect.

It was Dock who first addressed the youths.

"What's the problem here?" the ex-marine asked neutrally. In his youth, Dock would have been crazy enough to fight all three dealers, whether they had a gun or not. But at age forty-five, he recognized and respected how volatile the situation was.

"This piece of shit owes us money," one of the youths said to Dock. He pointed disdainfully at Kenyon. "He says you got the cash. Where is it?"

Negron and Dock studied Kenyon for the first time. He was a billboard of decay. Still wearing the same business suit Negron had seen him in four nights earlier, Kenyon was mysteriously missing his shoes and socks and, for some reason, was wearing a soiled T-shirt over his jacket. And the smell was awful. Obviously, it had been close to a week since Kenyon had last bathed.

"I'm sorry. I'm sorry. I fucked up," Kenyon said, openly sobbing. "Ray, help me, man. Please give me another chance."

One of the dealers slapped Kenyon on the back of the head.

"Shut the fuck up," he said. Then looking at Dock, he angrily asked, "Where the fuck's the money?"

Dock asked for a minute to get the cash. Leaving Negron alone in the alley with Kenyon, the marine returned to the car and apprised Gooden of the situation.

"Vincent's in pretty bad shape," Dock said. "I don't know what they're gonna do to him, but we better give 'em the money and get him out of here."

"I want to talk to them," Gooden said.

"Dwight, there's no need for that. Just give me one hundred dollars and we'll be right back with Vincent."

But Gooden insisted on negotiating face to face with Kenyon's captors. He and Dock returned to the alley, and Gooden took one look at Kenyon, then at the three dealers.

"What's the problem here?" he asked.

"You gonna make me repeat myself, motherfucker?" the biggest one said. "I ought to blow this motherfucker away 'cause he ain't worth all this trouble."

Gooden, sensing he'd been challenged, said, "Look, man, I'm strapped. You got a relative of mine and I want him back."

Those were two bold-faced lies, and Negron and Dock prayed Doc's bluff wouldn't be called. Gooden, of course, had no weapon, and he certainly wasn't Kenyon's relative. In fact, one of the group recognized the celebrity in their midst.

"Yo, man, you're Dwight Gooden. What are you doing with this piece of shit?" he said, poking Kenyon with the heel of his shoe.

"That's my cousin," Gooden said, clinging to his brazen lie. "You calling someone in my family a piece of shit? To my face?"

"We got no problem with you, Dwight. We know you're from the neighborhood," said the big dealer, apparently the leader. "We just want our money. This motherfucker's been using what he can't pay for."

Again, he slapped Kenyon on the head and asked, "Ain't that right?"

Kenyon, not looking up, made a small noise in his throat that sounded like a sob. Gooden decided his friend had suffered enough humiliation, and even though his notoriety had reduced the tension in the alley, it was time to pay the ransom. Gooden reached into his pocket and gave Negron two fifty-dollar bills. The agent walked over to the dealer and said, "This enough?"

The dealer considered the question for a moment, no doubt debating whether to demand more. He assumed Gooden was carrying plenty of cash, but he decided against it. The three turned and walked away, and, turning one last time to Kenyon, one of them said, "Don't come back."

In the car, Kenyon began to cry again, but Ron Dock cut him off. "Vincent, we're taking you to a place where you can get help," he said. "You have to go. Your life depends on it. Next time, you could end up dead."

But Kenyon protested, saying he needed nothing more than a shower and a meal and he would be fine. He was right on those two counts: Kenyon's body odor overpowered the little Subaru, and, judging by his breath, it seemed he hadn't eaten in a week. But Gooden told Kenyon, "If you don't get some help now, then everything you've been telling me these last few months was bullshit. It means recovery is a lie. If you can't admit you're sick, how do you expect me to do it?"

"Surrender to it, man. Surrender," Ron Dock said, almost shouting now. "Remember, if Custer had surrendered, he would've lived a long, long time. You're gonna die unless you surrender, Vincent."

The Subaru wound its way through downtown on a direct path to a recovery house called Prosperity Villa. Suddenly, there was silence in the car as Kenyon stopped protesting. Gooden put his arm around his fallen friend. Just as the car pulled up at the hospital, Gooden whispered to Kenyon, "We're here." There was no answer, but Gooden could feel the subtle shaking of Kenyon's shoulders as he softly cried.

BY EARLY AUGUST, Gooden was growing impatient with Acting Commissioner Selig's indecisiveness. "What else do I need to do?" Gooden asked himself as he reviewed his list of accomplishments over the summer. He was hosting a once-a-week radio show in Tampa, pulling in guests like Fred McGriff, Reds general manager Jim Bowden, Yogi Berra, and David Cone. Strawberry came on the show, too, and he and Doc talked wistfully about playing on the same team again. Strawberry was a Yankee now, but he had suffered through a long and bitter negotiation with George Steinbrenner, which worried Gooden.

Although Bill Goodstein had done an admirable job creating market interest for Strawberry, his subsequent dispute with Steinbrenner over contract language led Gooden to believe he was better off in Negron's exclusive care. Goodstein was furious with Negron for this unauthorized separation and accused him of having "stolen" Gooden. "Trust me, Ray, I will never forgive you for this," Goodstein said into the phone one August evening. And just like that, in the course of one phone call, the seventeen-year relationship between the agents ended.

"What Bill never understood is that Dwight's case wasn't like Darryl's," Negron said. "He didn't need to have a public fight over his contract, the way that Bill went to war over Darryl's. But Bill could never accept that. It was a terrible blow to his ego, to lose a client like that, and he blamed me. I wanted to explain that it was just a difference of opinion on strategy, but we never did speak again. There was too much anger on his part."

Negron had encouraged Gooden to take the lead in his efforts to gain reinstatement. In fact, Gooden had decided that when the time came, he would negotiate his own contract, part of a resolution to "take control of my life again," he said. "I was through letting other people make decisions for me. That's what was such a big part of the problem to begin with." But first, Gooden needed to hear from Selig.

Negron suggested a letter to the acting commissioner. Make it simple and direct, he said: ask for a chance to be heard in person, and let Selig decide for himself how far Gooden had come in his recovery. "Time's running out, Doc. At this point you have nothing to lose," Negron said.

So Doc sat before his computer and composed a letter telling Selig everything he'd done over the summer, all the reasons he thought made sense for reinstatement. Gooden also promised to respect any decision Selig made. What Gooden didn't tell Selig was that his fastball was better than ninety miles per hour now and that he could certainly help some team get to the play-offs.

"What do you think about the Yankees, Doc?" Negron asked after the letter was sent.

"What about 'em?" Gooden asked with a smile. The attraction to the Bronx was obvious, especially now that Strawberry was a Yankee. Also, George Steinbrenner was a Tampa neighbor, and what better way for Gooden to tweak the Mets than to join their cross-town rivals? It wasn't even a question of money; it was about proving to the world that Dwight Gooden, recovering addict, could still be some kind of role model.

There was only one obstacle, and that was baseball's own image problem. Attendance was down nearly 23 percent in the wake of the strike, and all of the public's frustration toward major leaguers that had built up over the years was now manifesting itself in ballparks all over the country. But it was even worse than no one liking ballplayers; no one cared. The last thing Selig needed was to stick his neck out for Gooden, who less than a year earlier seemed so lost in his addiction.

If only there hadn't been so many positive tests in the fall of '94, if only there hadn't been so much poststrike animosity to melt, maybe Selig would have taken a gamble on Gooden. But not in 1995. He sent back a happy, encouraging note, telling Gooden he was on the right path and that all he had to do was keep working hard. Gooden read the letter three times to make sure he understood the unspoken message from the acting commissioner: carefully wrapped in all the pleasantries was the verdict he dreaded. No reinstatement. Not in 1995.

Gooden called Negron and relayed the bad news. "We're done," he told the agent. "They won't give me a shot."

"Well, Dwight, we knew it might turn out this way. You have to stay strong. You can't fall now. Fact is, you've got to be stronger than ever."

Negron was obviously worried about depression and anger taking Gooden down. But at least Selig's letter said Gooden would be unconditionally reinstated at the end of the regular season, October 1, without any further petitioning. That meant for the entire month of October, Gooden would be baseball's only free agent, since the normal free-agency period wouldn't begin until after the World Series. But first things first: Gooden had to overcome his disappointment.

That week, at an NA meeting, Gooden told the group he couldn't understand how others still had control over his life, how those who didn't understand recovery were judging him on his. Every day in September, Gooden watched the Yankees on TV, wondering what it would be like to be part of the pennant race in the Bronx. The Yankees were in the midst of an incredible stretch, winning twenty-four of thirty-one and qualifying for the postseason for the first time since 1981. And all Gooden could do was watch.

He'd decided that his future was with either the Yankees or the Marlins. Both choices had strong appeal for Gooden: the Yankees were in New York, where he grew up as a ballplayer and where he still had unfinished business. But playing for the Marlins would mean being closer to home and thus being closer to his family, especially his father, as well as being a teammate of his nephew, Gary Sheffield.

Gooden ran through the choices: he knew the National League, so being a Yankee meant learning at least three hundred new scouting reports. As a National Leaguer Gooden would still be able to hit; as a Yankee he would surrender his bat to the designated hitter. As a National Leaguer he would be able to walk into Shea Stadium, stand on the mound, and issue a silent "Take that!" to Dallas Green; the American League offered no such direct revenge.

Then why did the image of a Yankee uniform keep tugging at him? Maybe it was, as Negron said, that "no team in baseball has the Yankees' tradition. There's something special about wearing pinstripes." Negron was prejudiced, of course, having been linked to the Yankees since 1973. Negron was just a sixteen-year-old then, "a punk," in his own words, who was caught spray-painting the walls outside the stadium by none other than George Steinbrenner himself.

"George must've been going to the airport or something because he was getting in his limousine, just about to drive off when he saw me and my friends and stopped the car," Negron said. "They all ran, but George caught me. He grabbed me by my shirt and pulled me into the front door of the ballpark. I thought for sure I was headed to the police holding cell they have downstairs. I was thinking, 'Christ, I'm getting arrested, what am I going to tell my father?' "

Steinbrenner had a different plan for Negron, however. Instead of turning him over to the police, he gave the youth to clubhouse man Pete Sheehy, an old, wrinkled shell who was as much a part of Yankee history as Ruth or Gehrig or Mantle. Sheehy had been the equipment manager since the 1920s and was respected by every player who ever entered his domain. "Pete, do something with this kid," Steinbrenner said, shoving Negron in the old man's direction.

That's how Negron eventually became the Yankee bat boy. And that's how he soon forged a relationship with Billy Martin that would last until the day the legendary Yankee manager died in 1989. Negron would become an accomplished college shortstop at New York Tech and even spend two seasons in the Pirates' system. But always, he returned to the Yankees, serving as their first-ever videotape director and then becoming Reggie Jackson's personal aide. In fact, one of Negron's favorite pastimes was telling Gooden that when Jackson hit his third home run in game six of the 1977 World Series, it was Negron who pushed Reggie out of the dugout to wave to the crowd.

At first, the story entertained Gooden, but when he realized the agent would repeat it every day, Gooden soon prohibited it. "Stop, I surrender, whatever you want, just don't tell that story anymore, Ray," he would say with a laugh. Still, Negron's loyalty to the Yankees had made an impression on Gooden. And on October 5, Doc found himself face to face with Steinbrenner in a Tampa restaurant.

There was no direct negotiating that day, only Steinbrenner talking about recovery. "I've got a cousin who had a problem with alcohol, so I understand what addiction is about, Dwight," the Yankee owner said. "I know how it can ruin a life, but what I respect about you is that you haven't given up. You've worked very hard to regain control of your life."

Steinbrenner told Gooden that if he signed with the Yankees, he would answer to pitching coach Billy Connors and explained how Connors had once worked with an undiscovered talent with the Chicago Cubs named Greg Maddux. It was Connors who taught Maddux his nearly unhittable slider, and Connors could do the same for Gooden, too.

Then it was Gooden's turn to talk.

"Dwight, tell me about your recovery," Steinbrenner said. "What happens when you have an urge to do drugs? When do you get them? And how often?"

"Well, I can't say for sure when they happen; there's no set time or pattern," Gooden said. "But when I start to feel an urge, I'll call Ray, or my sponsor, a guy named Ron Dock, and they can talk me through it. Ron reminds me of what the result of using drugs will be, how I could throw everything away I've been building for in the last few months."

Gooden went on to describe the NA meetings in St. Petersburg and how, for the first time, the addicts he exchanged stories with weren't millionaires but just street people. Steinbrenner listened, fascinated. "I believed that Dwight was being honest with me that day," he said, and, because of that, the Yankee owner was convinced Gooden deserved a second life in the major leagues. After all, if Steinbrenner had rescued Darryl Strawberry, what reason was there to say no to Gooden, especially if the reports of a ninety-mile-per-hour fastball were accurate?

The next time Gooden and Negron met with Steinbrenner, the owner's tone was more businesslike. In fact, George was in a barely contained state of rage, since the Yankees had just lost game five of the divisional play-off series to the Mariners. Steinbrenner decided he needed pitching help and more than ever was determined to sign Gooden. Steinbrenner had heard all about Gooden's private audition with the Marlins in late September, when he threw for fifteen minutes, his fastball so impressive General Manager Dave Dombrowski was hooked right there.

The Marlins treated Gooden to a night in their luxury boxes, as he sat next to owner Wayne Huizenga during a game against the Phillies. "We'll see you in spring training, Doc," the owner said with a wink after the last out. Until he had met with Steinbrenner, Gooden was actually leaning toward Florida and told former teammate Gary Carter, now a broadcaster with the Marlins, "This is where I want to be."

But that was before Steinbrenner made Gooden the epicenter of his business world. "There is no team in baseball that can match the Yankees for history and pride," Steinbrenner said. Gooden looked at Negron. Now he knew where the speeches came from. "And I want you to be part of that, Dwight. I think you can be a Yankee for a long time. I know you've talked to some other clubs, the Marlins, for instance. Go out and compare the figures they've given you with what I'm about to suggest and let's see if we can work this thing out."

Steinbrenner paused a moment, then said, "I'd like to pay you about one million dollars, and we could possibly add an option year, maybe two. Then we'll go from there." Gooden nodded, letting the numbers sink in. He'd brought his father along with Negron, and now the three decided they'd heard enough for one day. "Give me twenty-four hours," Gooden said. On the way home, the three discussed the offer. The Marlins had actually offered more money, $1.5 million, but without a promise for a second or third year. Gooden decided he'd take less money the first year, as long as there was security on the back end. When they arrived in St. Petersburg the pitcher and the agent developed a counterproposal, which, with incentives, would pay Gooden base salaries of $1 million in 1996, $2 million in 1997, and $3 million in 1998. The incentives would be primarily tied to the number of innings Gooden pitched. He decided it was fair to give the Yankees that protection, and Gooden also decided it was only right that the options to pick up his contract for '97 and '98 would be the Yankees'. Gooden, however, asked for a $300,000 payout if the Yankees exercised that option in either the second or third year.

The next day, Steinbrenner brought his attorney, David Sussman, to the Bay Harbor Inn and made a formal offer: in 1996, the Yankees would pay Gooden $850,000, then $1.8 million for 1997. Gooden listened to the incentives offered, which were unsatisfactory. He also wanted a third year added to the contract.

"Mr. Steinbrenner, we have a counterproposal for you," Gooden said, and handed a typewritten offer to the owner and his attorney. For the next fifteen minutes, Steinbrenner didn't say a word, simply reading and rereading. He would occasionally look up at Gooden, his small, dark eyes slicing right through the pitcher. Doc later said, "I was sweating like crazy, waiting for him to say something. I realized that being a businessman wasn't easy."

Finally, Steinbrenner took a deep breath and said, "Okay, I'll pay two million for the second year if I pick up the option, and I'll give you three million for the third year, but I'm not paying $300,000 for a buyout."

"Well, I'll say yes to $850,000 for next season. Look, you gave Darryl $650,000 for three months' work, I'll be a bargain at $850,000," Gooden said.

Steinbrenner nodded. "Fine, you've got the $300,000 buyout, but I'm not accepting some of your incentives. You want an extra $200,000 just for pitching a hundred and twenty-five innings? That's ridiculous. And I'm not paying $250,000 if you win the Cy Young. You either win it or you don't."

"Mr. Steinbrenner, the White Sox offered $500,000."

Steinbrenner doubted that but nevertheless relented just slightly. "I'll give you $50,000."

There was another pause among the men. This time, the silence was hopeful.

Gooden extended his hand. "You've got a deal," Doc said, almost sprinting out of the room to the closest pay phone.

"Dad," Gooden said breathlessly. "I'm a Yankee."

10

A BRONX TALE

THE JUNE 20 press conference in Tampa had barely ended when George Steinbrenner whispered to Darryl Strawberry, "Just get yourself ready and we'll see you in New York in a week or two." Little did Darryl know that a week would stretch to forty-four days, during which time Steinbrenner tried to renegotiate the contract, then reword the language, all the while refusing to pay Strawberry even his minor-league salary.

Bill Goodstein had always considered Steinbrenner a friend, but the longer the owner extended Strawberry's minor-league rehab assignment, the more it seemed to the agent that "George must consider Darryl an eighteen-sixty-three slave." Within days after White House drug czar Lee Brown criticized the deal, Steinbrenner called Goodstein at his Manhattan office and said, "Look, I've taken a tremendous hit on this thing. I've got to have a few extra provisions in the contract or else we're not going to do the deal. I'm having my lawyers work on it; you'll get a chance to look it over."

It took twenty-two days for Steinbrenner to get back to Goodstein, and the lawyer discovered the "little things" the owner referred to were potentially devastating to Strawberry. First, the Yankees demanded that a third of Darryl's salary, more than $200,000, be donated to charity. Furthermore, Strawberry was to designate another third of his remaining income to a trust for his children, and the club insisted that the entire family, not just Strawberry himself, be subject to drug tests. And finally, the Yankees demanded that a bank officer at Citibank be empowered to coordinate Strawberry's payments to the IRS as well as his alimony and support to his ex-wife, Lisa.

Goodstein was furious. "Let me ask you something, George," he said. "You realize, of course, that Darryl owes the government over three hundred thousand dollars. If he gives two hundred thousand dollars to charity, how is he supposed to pay his back taxes?"

It was a fair question, and, ultimately, Steinbrenner would back down. But Darryl and Charisse were slowly learning that being a Yankee didn't necessarily mean being happy. Charisse was particularly incensed over the drug-testing clause in the revised contract, saying, "It was so insulting, Darryl and I couldn't believe it. This contract had nothing to do with the kids. Why couldn't they just leave them out of it?"

But worst of all for Strawberry was Steinbrenner's delay in paying him his minor-league salary. It was a mere $10,000, yet Goodstein was forced to call Yankee attorney David Sussman several times to ask for the check. Goodstein would later admit it was a miscalculation on his part to accept a separate minor-league payment clause in the contract, but he said,

"There was no reason to believe George was going to let Darryl linger that long in the minor leagues. I took him at his word, which was: the Yankees signed Darryl to play for the Yankees, not the Columbus Clippers."

Without an income, Strawberry's financial situation deteriorated badly. He was unable to secure a loan from a New York bank despite Goodstein's round-the-clock efforts, and, as a result, even paying the most routine household bills, like power and electric, became touch-and-go.

The check finally arrived in mid-July, but it left Goodstein feeling terribly guilty. Had he led Darryl down the wrong path? The lawyer wondered if the White Sox would have been a better choice, even for less money. Yet Strawberry told Goodstein, "Don't fight so much, Bill, it'll all work out." To the press, Strawberry was just as tranquil. Even though he was hitting over .300 for the Clippers, blasting home runs at a rate of one every three games, he refused to snap. "Whatever George wants to do with me is fine," Strawberry said. "Look where I was three months ago. Man, I'm just lucky to be playing again."

But back in New York, Goodstein's Strawberry-related workload suffocated his entire practice. Adding to the problem were the phone calls from an anonymous woman from California, who was demanding $300,000 or else she would reveal that Strawberry had been violating his aftercare program and house arrest by committing adultery. The threats seemed real, and Goodstein was forced to call in the FBI. Agents tapped the phones in Goodstein's office, and, when she called again, she repeated her threat. It was extortion, a felony, and, under the FBI's instructions, Goodstein agreed to pay the money. One day in June, Goodstein arranged to have the woman meet him in his office, where two agents promptly arrested her.

Living under house arrest made Strawberry a vulnerable target, but he regarded it as just an inconvenience. In fact, it wasn't an altogether unpleasant experience. Before his promotion to the big leagues, Strawberry was given Arthur Richman, the Yankees' executive vice president, as a roommate. They led a remarkably dull life together. "I didn't do much except read, talk to my wife on the phone, and go to the park early, which was great. It cleared my head," Strawberry said. Richman, whose assignment was supposed to last no more than one week, said, "Darryl did absolutely nothing. It was the most boring two months I ever spent."

Sooner or later, however, the Yankees would have to relent and summon Strawberry. He remembered watching them on TV in late July and noticing, "They seemed so dead, like they don't have a leader." In the old days, such a proclamation would have landed Darryl on the back pages, but an older, humbler Strawberry meant no insult by it in 1995. Strawberry just couldn't understand why Steinbrenner signed him in the first place if all he was being asked to do was hit home runs off Triple-A pitching.

Goodstein was preparing to file a grievance with the Players Association and at one point, in a face-to-face meeting with Steinbrenner at the stadium, called the Yankee owner "an asshole." In response, Steinbrenner stormed out of the room, yelling, "You've gone too far this time, Goodstein." But none of the hostility ever reached Strawberry, who kept proving that he hadn't lost any of his bat speed. Reliever Joe Ausanio, who spent much of the summer of '95 shuttling between the Bronx and the International League, said after watching Strawberry hit, "It was like putting a man up there against a bunch of children."

Strawberry had no way of knowing that his arrival would cause roster problems for Buck Showalter, who was locked in a personal war with Steinbrenner. Although Showalter liked Strawberry initially, that was before the Yankees acquired switch-hitting designated hitter Ruben Sierra from the Oakland A's. It would be Showalter's burden to find at-bats for his new designated hitter/right fielder. Showalter wrestled with his options: Strawberry's natural position was right field, but Paul O'Neill made it clear he wanted no part of switching to left, where Luis Polonia and Gerald Williams shared playing time. And Sierra, with a huge three-year contract, was unmovable.

In fact, Strawberry's arrival on August 4 had every possibility of turning into a disaster, especially since the team was forced to release Polonia to make room for him. But Strawberry was embraced by an unlikely supporter, who, ultimately, made it possible for the former Met to survive in the Bronx. It was Don Mattingly—the same man who openly criticized replacement player Dave Pavlas's presence in the clubhouse—who told the world, "Strawberry is welcome here."

"I did that because I've always liked Darryl, and I believe that people deserve a second chance in life," Mattingly said. "Yeah, I knew what I was doing, going public with some of my statements. But I wanted my teammates and the fans to know that this was a guy who was trying to build his life again. Who are we to say no to a man trying to do his best? I thought it was the right thing to do."

O'Neill took Mattingly's cue and also endorsed Strawberry. "As long as he proves that he's still capable of swinging the bat, then I have no problem with Darryl Strawberry being a Yankee," O'Neill said. "What happened to him in the past is none of my business or anyone else's. We're here to win a pennant, and if he can help, then he can be a part of this team."

Not surprisingly, Strawberry took a locker next to Mattingly's, and it wasn't unusual to see them chatting for long stretches before games. One day in early September, Mattingly approached Darryl and said, "Straw, you want my locker next year?"

Strawberry may or may not have known that Mattingly's corner locker belonged historically to Yankee captains and, before him, was Ron Guidry's living space. Strawberry was somewhat surprised by the offer, though, since it implied that Mattingly wasn't returning to the Yankees in 1996.

"Nah, Donnie, George don't want me back here. Buck won't even play me," Strawberry said.

"Well, someone's gotta be here next year. Might as well be you, Straw," Mattingly said. "I ain't coming back, that's for sure."

Strawberry shrugged, assuming it was Mattingly's bad back that was clouding his teammate's judgment. But Mattingly was telling the truth that day, as he ultimately declined the Yankees' offer for arbitration and thus ended his fourteen-year association with the club. Mattingly was a good clubhouse neighbor for Strawberry, as was Steve Howe, another recovering addict. After the season, Strawberry told Gooden how much he liked the hyperactive, gum-chewing, chain-smoking Howe. "Doc, he's the craziest guy you'll ever meet. I love him," Strawberry said to Gooden. Still, there was no replacing a ghost from Darryl's Met past, now only a few feet away in the Yankee clubhouse: David Cone.

"George, look at you!" Strawberry said, using an old Met nickname for Cone, in honor of George Brett. Cone was once a Kansas City Royal, where he learned about running a hard night life from the master, Brett. The two players only had to exchange looks to realize how far they had come since Shea in the mid-eighties. Cone, once the wildest of the wild-side Mets, was now baseball's premier hired gun, having been traded three times in three years during pennant races. He was also one of the Players Association's most articulate spokesmen during the strike and, after a seventeen-win season in 1995, on his way to becoming baseball's richest pitcher, signing with the Yankees a guaranteed three-year deal worth $19 million.

It seemed like so many years ago when Strawberry and Cone were two young, out-of-control Mets. Teammates will never forget their outrageous joke one day in 1989, when, in the visitors' clubhouse at Wrigley Field, Strawberry used his genitals to stir a bowl of ice cream. Cone, noting that his teammate needed to "cool off," poured a beer into the overheated bowl.

Now, wealthy, married, and responsible, it seemed Cone's greatest vice was smoking cigarettes. "Man, I've got to stop," he said with a laugh one September at the stadium. "I used to limit the smokes only to the ballpark, but it's getting worse all the time." There were many ex-Mets who found it fashionable to bash Strawberry after he left New York; certainly after the *Sports Illustrated* story in February, Darryl had hardly any friends among the Shea alumni. But Cone remained loyal to Strawberry, and he made it no secret, stating, "I will do anything I can to help him and protect him. Sure, we were wild together in the old days. I did things. Darryl did things. We all did. But they're over now. As far as I'm concerned, it's in the past. I look at him now, and I see a guy who's sincere about starting over. That's good enough for me. Just watch him take batting practice and tell me that isn't a career worth salvaging."

Cone was right: it became a daily ritual at the stadium to watch Strawberry take batting practice at about 5:30 P.M. The ballpark would come to a stop as everyone—teammates, coaches, reporters, even stadium workers—would admire one line drive after another screaming into the seats. It wasn't unusual for Strawberry to reach the upper deck, and, on his good days, he averaged about seven batting-practice home runs for every ten swings.

"Jesus Christ, are you shitting me?" General Manager Gene Michael mumbled to himself after a Strawberry blast landed in the monuments in center field, some 450 feet away. "Look at that guy. Hey, Buck, you watching that?"

Showalter didn't miss much, especially when it came to his Yankees. The little manager knew that Strawberry was still a powerful man. Buck asked hitting coach Rick Down for his opinion on Strawberry's unusual batting style, whether the coiling of the front foot and the long loop in his swing would hinder Darryl against ninety-mile-per-hour fastballs. Down said no, explaining, "He's still very quick getting the bat into the strike zone. That's what matters most. Straw is long with the swing only after he's made contact, but there's nothing wrong with that. He's still fine."

What bothered Showalter was Strawberry's defense. At times, the manager confided to friends that he feared for Darryl's safety. "Jesus, he looks awful sometimes, like he's lost his hand-eye coordination," Showalter said. It was the worst kind of catch-22 for both parties. The longer Strawberry went without playing the outfield, the rustier his skills became. And the less capable Strawberry became in the outfield, the less likely it was that Showalter would use him there.

But one thing was certain: Strawberry was no trouble in the clubhouse. Showalter had prepared for the worst, having heard from Tommy Lasorda just after the Yankees signed the right fielder. "Be ready," Lasorda had said, "for more distractions than you ever counted on."

Even Ruben Sierra's private chats with Strawberry, in which he told the right fielder he was being mistreated by the Yankees, failed to evoke any anger. "With you and me together, we have one of the most powerful lineups in baseball. And they don't even let you play," Sierra said. On three occasions in September, Strawberry met with Showalter, but, instead of complaining about his at-bats, he told the manager, "Don't worry about me, I'm fine. I'll be ready when you need me."

Surely Strawberry knew he was being closely watched by the Yankee front office. And if he didn't, then Goodstein was quick to remind him. At times, the lawyer even counseled Strawberry not to speak to the press. "You can only hurt yourself by answering a lot of questions, Darryl," Goodstein said one day. "It's better off that you say nothing at all." If ever there was a barometer of Strawberry's maturity, it was this refusal to be provoked.

Strawberry eventually earned the right to speak his mind following a dramatic home run against Erik Hanson of the Red Sox on September 10. Strawberry was part of a three-game sweep of division-leading Boston, and before the game he whispered to a reporter, "Watch me, I'm going deep tonight." Hanson seemed a perfect fit for Strawberry's looping uppercut: a hard thrower whose fastball, despite its ninety-mile-per-hour-plus velocity, was nevertheless straight enough to track.

In all his years in baseball, Strawberry was at his best under pressure. Davey Johnson used to say, "Darryl loved to play to the moment," which is what made for many memorable moments in his career. Not many Met fans could forget the massive home run he hit against the Cardinals' Ken Dayley in the final hours of the 1985 pennant race, a blast that hit the clock at Busch Stadium and gave the Mets a 1–0 win in eleven innings. Strawberry still believes the game-three home run against Nolan Ryan in the 1986 play-offs against Houston was his most productive homer, although it was Strawberry's bloop single in the ninth inning of game six that led to the three-run rally that turned the game into a sixteen-inning marathon.

Moments such as these made it possible to see Strawberry's career as a miniature tragedy. So much talent, so much of it traded away for a cheap high. At thirty-two, Strawberry had veered off the road so many thought would lead to Cooperstown, but he at least was willing to understand that "the last few years of my career can be dedicated toward finishing strong. Doing things I should've been doing all along."

The home run off Hanson was pure eighties nostalgia—a line drive that was history the moment it left Strawberry's bat. He circled the bases in slow motion, not necessarily to gloat over the Red Sox but to savor the sensation of being important again. "It's nice to be respected. It's been a long time since I had that feeling," he said. Showalter was told that, once again, Strawberry had passed up an opportunity to complain about his diminished playing time. The manager shook his head and told a reporter, "You know, I really wouldn't mind having Darryl back here next year."

Not only was Strawberry a clubhouse conformist but there hadn't been the slightest hint of trouble in his recovery. Even the Yankees' trip to the West Coast, which Goodstein feared would tempt Darryl, came and went without incident. It wasn't drugs that worried the lawyer but the decade-old itch to empty his wallet to friends and family. "That was probably the hardest part of all, getting Darryl to understand the need to curtail his spending and to say no to people who ask him for money," Goodstein said.

The Yankees made sure they identified the parasites who historically preyed on Strawberry. Those were the terms of his agreement with Steinbrenner—the complete and oppressive control over his personal life. The man responsible for such surveillance was a former Drug Enforcement Agency chieftain named James Williams, whose twenty-one-year history with the government included undercover stints in the Caribbean, Mexico, Argentina, Egypt, Italy, and Bolivia. Before he retired in 1994, Williams had as his final assignment working with the Organized Crime Task Force in New York City, tracking the flow of drugs into the metropolitan area.

Monitoring Darryl Strawberry seemed like a vacation by comparison, but Williams nevertheless enjoyed his time with the outfielder. "I came to realize Darryl was trustworthy," he said. "Every time we checked on him, we found he was complying with the terms of his house arrest. And, I mean, to the letter. A large part of it was based on the honor system, but there was no reason to believe Darryl was cutting corners. I think he learned his lesson."

Yet Williams was privy to the growing frustration Strawberry felt in the final weeks of the season as he virtually disappeared from the lineup and from the play-offs against the Mariners, when he didn't start a single game. "Darryl basically felt that he was getting abused," said Williams, who noticed a series of small, but unmistakable changes in Strawberry's demeanor. Suddenly, he was wearing louder clothes and more jewelry, and he had returned to brandishing a diamond-studded Rolex. Strawberry seemed more difficult to talk to, often drifting in some self-induced fog.

"Man, it was hard to understand what the Yankees were thinking because they had to know I could still swing the bat," Strawberry said. "I mean, they signed me for a reason, right? To play. So why wouldn't they let me play? I didn't do anything wrong, like so many people thought I would. Folks thought I would run my mouth, or do drugs or something, but none of that happened. Sometimes it would frustrate me."

"That's exactly what we were worried about," Williams said. During the play-offs, Strawberry left the Yankees' hotel early one afternoon, choosing to take a taxi to the ballpark. That didn't constitute any violation of his house arrest, but it was out of character for Strawberry, who normally rode with Williams. When the former agent arrived at The Kingdome, he saw Strawberry talking to a group of people in a late-model Mercedes. Strawberry later told Williams they were friends of the family, but that didn't stop the agent from running a complete background check. It turned out Strawberry was telling the truth: the friends had no criminal record and posed no threat. But Williams said, "With Darryl, you could never be too careful. You never knew who was out there trying to influence him, whether they were good guys or bad."

Strawberry didn't mind the scrutiny, but sometimes, he said, "It seemed like the only times the team paid attention to me was off the field." Indeed, as the Yankees' season ended in Seattle, Strawberry felt more removed than ever. He had had just two at-bats in the entire play-off series. In the aftermath of the Yankees' dramatic 6–5, eleven-inning loss to the Mariners in game five, in which the New Yorkers were only five outs away from a 4–2 victory, Strawberry stood alone in the clubhouse, feeling betrayed by 1995 and wondering if 1996 would be any less gray.

"Some people just don't understand what I can do," he said, nodding vaguely in the direction of Showalter's office. "We got guys on the team who aren't producing, but no one trusts me. I don't get it." Strawberry's observation needed no translation: he'd been passed over for the light-hitting Dion James, whose defensive superiority over Strawberry was negated by his inability even to get the ball out of the infield in five plate appearances in game five. Showalter said, "I didn't want to run the risk of Darryl embarrassing himself out there in the outfield, and, to be honest, there was too much at stake at that point to start experimenting." Still, James finished the series with just one hit in twelve at-bats, and Strawberry seemed close to his breaking point as his teammates slowly packed their bags and prepared for a long charter flight home.

Mattingly's eyes were red and moist as he talked about the Yankees' demise. "At least we gave it everything we had. We have nothing to be ashamed of," he said. David Cone admitted it would take several months before he could erase the image of a 3-2 split-finger fastball he threw to Doug Strange with the bases loaded in the eighth inning that allowed the tying run to score. And George Steinbrenner issued a subtle but nevertheless clear threat against Showalter for allowing Cone to throw 147 pitches.

All around the room, the Yankees were suffering. Their grief was not unlike what the 1988 Mets experienced after losing game seven of the NLCS to the Dodgers, when Strawberry cried openly. But against the Mariners, Strawberry could find no tears. He felt that much of an outsider. Perhaps Steinbrenner sensed Strawberry's alienation because he pulled his troubled outfielder aside and whispered in his ear, "Listen, Darryl, I know what you're thinking. But don't worry because next year you won't have this problem. I want you back here, and I want you to play every day."

Strawberry took Steinbrenner at his word, and two weeks later he was in Tampa, participating in the Yankees' mini-camp. It was a football-type training session in which Strawberry was supposed to receive a crash course in playing left field. The club had only two weeks to decide whether to pick up his option; by November 1, the Yankees would either have to pay him $1.8 million for the 1996 season or else buy him out for $175,000.

The days were a blur of fly balls, long home runs from the batting cage, and, afterward, solitude in a hotel two blocks from the Yankee complex. "What else do they want me to do?" Strawberry asked in exasperation as the club withheld its decision. It didn't help the outfielder that Showalter was on his way to another job, managing the expansion Diamond-Backs in Arizona, and General Manager Gene Michael was deposed by an internal coup. Replacing them were Joe Torre and Bob Watson.

Watson's appointment was particularly troubling news for Strawberry. Watson had just served as the Astros' general manager, and Goodstein recalled that, during the months before signing with the Yankees, Strawberry was offered to Houston.

"Not interested," Watson said bluntly. Before hanging up the phone, he added, "Absolutely not." Apparently, Watson wasn't any more impressed with Strawberry now that he was his property. The Yankees asked Strawberry for an extra month to decide his fate and further requested he play left field for the Santurce Crabbers in the Puerto Rican winter league.

Strawberry had lost nearly all his patience by now, and it took a considerable amount of coaxing from Goodstein before he acquiesced. As it was, Strawberry left the Yankee mini-camp a day early, checking out of his hotel, walking into the airport, and booking a nonstop flight from Tampa to Los Angeles. It was Strawberry's way of telling Steinbrenner and

Watson just what he thought of their delaying tactics. "You watch," Strawberry said. "They're not gonna keep me. They've had it in for me all along. The only reason I'm even going to Puerto Rico is so other teams can have a chance to see what I can do."

In all, Strawberry played just nine games with the Crabbers, hitting .355 with six home runs and ten RBIs. With Strawberry in the lineup, Santurce climbed from last place to first, and team owner Reinaldo Paniagua said, "Darryl proved to us that he still has a lot of baseball left in him." But that still wasn't enough to satisfy the Yankees.

All the while, they were planning on finding another left-handed power hitter, seemingly achieving that goal when the Mariners' Tino Martinez was acquired in exchange for left-hander Sterling Hitchcock and third baseman Russell Davis. On December 2, the Yankees made the decision final: they wrote Strawberry a check for $175,000 and bid him farewell.

Strawberry took the news badly and, for the first time ever, spoke of an early retirement. "Maybe it's just not meant to be," he said. "I tried so hard to prove that I was worthy of another chance, but some people can't get it out of their heads that I should be punished. All I ever wanted to do was play ball."

Those words reminded a reporter of the 1985 season, when Strawberry had thirty-nine home runs and ninety-nine RBIs. Even though the Mets had been eliminated by the Cards in the final week of the season, there was still time for Strawberry to reach the forty-homer and one-hundred RBI milestones. But he declined to play in the final games because he said the Cardinals had rendered them meaningless. And besides, Strawberry said, "There'll be plenty of time in my career to get to one hundred RBIs."

It turned out that Strawberry misused the years, ignoring them as they whispered by, all of them too fast, until one day he realized he was thirty-three. On his good days, Strawberry can avoid thinking about the home runs he never hit. But there are moments when the same, sad question lingers. "Man, imagine if I'd gotten sober ten years ago," Strawberry said, lowering his eyes.

Time, scorned, never forgives.

11

DOC REDUX

THE OCEAN WAVES rolled over the beach in steady, pleasing rhythms. Even in a hotel room ten stories above, the sound was soothing enough to put Ray Negron to sleep. But not Dwight Gooden, who sat in a chair in the San Juan Holiday Inn, reading the Puerto Rican winter-league schedule, scouting out his potential opponents.

"Hey, Ray, who's this team, the Libres?" Gooden wanted to know. Negron hadn't opened his eyes yet, but he was now awake.

"What are you talking about?" the agent said wearily.

"The Libres. I'm pitching against them next week," Gooden said. "Who do they have in the lineup?"

Gooden had been dependent on Negron the moment he signed with the San Juan Senators in November, a one-month tune-up that was part of his contract with the Yankees. Gooden said, "It felt great to be going somewhere again, actually competing," but playing in Puerto Rico had its surcharge. First and foremost, the pitcher didn't speak a word of Spanish and needed Negron to act as a twenty-four-hour-a-day translator.

"Oh, the Libres. Jesus. You're starting against them?" Negron said, suddenly sitting up.

"Yeah, I got them on Monday," Gooden said, startled by Negron's response.

"Fuck, they got this cleanup hitter, Martinez is his name I think. Big dude, about six-four, two hundred and forty pounds," Negron said. "Jesus, man, you're not ready for him. He's got a quick bat, great plate coverage, doesn't chase out of the strike zone. He can hit a fastball a mile. And he hates Americans who come down here to play every winter."

"That right?" Gooden said, eyes narrowing slightly. "I'll buzz him once, right by his head, see how he likes that."

Negron shook his head. "Dwight, I don't know. Maybe you ought to pitch Tuesday against Santurce."

"Fuck that!" Gooden said, exploding. "You think I can't handle the Libres? You're supposed to be my agent, man. Go ahead, say it, you think the Libres are gonna kick my ass, don't you?"

Negron had, for several minutes, tried to contain his laughter, but it had become impossible. Seeing Gooden in full rage convinced the agent that Gooden's competitive urges were fully restored and that he was, professionally, as healthy as he'd ever seen him. It was a defining moment for Gooden, and Negron wanted to tell his pitcher exactly that. But first, Negron had to compose himself.

"Listen, you idiot, you're not pitching Monday. And the reason is, there's no game," Negron said. "Libre isn't a team. It means 'free' in Spanish, open, as in day off. It's San Juan's off day."

Gooden paused for a moment, then burst into laughter himself. "You got me, Ray. That's what I get for coming to Puerto Rico with a Puerto Rican agent," he said.

It turned out to be a satisfactory three-week stay. Gooden pitched three times, never allowing more than one earned run in each of his five-inning stints. His fastball was clocked at ninety-one miles per hour, and, more important, his new-found slider seemed to be effective. Yankees adviser Billy Connors, who commuted to San Juan from Tampa on the days Gooden threw, said, "There's no question he still has it." And when the club subsequently signed David Cone and Kenny Rogers as free agents, Gooden became the number three starter on what appeared to be a potent Yankee team.

In fact, Gooden had become such an important part of the Yankee tapestry that, one month later, George Steinbrenner asked him to be the featured guest at the club's Christmas event. It was a yearly party thrown for Tampa's inner-city children, and it was important to Steinbrenner that it be perfect.

Since Gooden agreed to be in Tampa for the party by 9:30 A.M., he told Negron he'd pick him up at 8:00 and, on the way over, he'd take his drug test, which he was required to do three times a week. At 8:15, however, Gooden had not arrived at Negron's house. At 8:30 Negron was convinced his world was coming to a horrible end.

"Dwight had never, ever been late for anything in the past year we've been together. If he said he'd be somewhere at eight, he'd be there at seven-forty-five," Negron said. "So when it got to be eight-fifteen, I was scared." After all these months, could Gooden have gone down again?

Negron paced the floor in his office, almost frantic, and by 8:40 he was wondering how he could explain Gooden's absence to Steinbrenner. But what could Negron say? The agent knew Gooden had been awarded just one chance by the Yankees, and it would be his last in baseball. All the hard work was in jeopardy, replaced by a world without baseball. Negron tried to imagine how Gooden would fare, permanently removed from the sport. The thought was too dark to entertain. Negron put his head on the desk and felt himself starting to cry.

He was alone for several minutes when the doorbell rang. It was Gooden, smiling.

"What's the matter, man? Your eyes are all red," the pitcher said.

"I . . . I overslept," Negron stammered.

"Then I'm glad I didn't call you this morning. I went to get the car washed," he said. "Come on, we gotta get to Tampa."

"What about the drug test?" Negron said, silently bracing for the worst.

"Doctor said to come by this afternoon. Eight-thirty's too early," Gooden said. The two got into Doc's car, off to Tampa, and Negron did his best to act normally. During the ride, though, Gooden thought he saw a tear in Negron's eye. It was probably just the light, Doc thought.

12

ALONE AGAIN . . .
NATURALLY

THE VOICE ON the other end of the phone was thick with grief, even through long-distance. Darryl Strawberry had been up for nearly twenty-four straight hours, and, even then, the tears didn't stop flowing. On January 13, his agent, Bill Goodstein, died suddenly in his office of a heart attack, leaving Darryl not only without a representative but without the most permanent father figure he'd had since his teens.

"Bill meant everything to me. He was the reason I turned my life around," Strawberry said. Goodstein handled the Strawberrys' finances, their taxes, even refereed through the natural turbulence in their marriage. Charisse estimated Goodstein called "four or five times a day, most of the time just to chat and not just talk business. Darryl and I are both devastated by this."

In his final days, Goodstein devoted all his efforts to get Strawberry one more—perhaps one last—contract.

He seemed to be making progress with the Red Sox, although General Manager Dan Duquette certainly wasn't offering much money—less than $1 million—and made it clear there was plenty of competition with Strawberry at the designated hitter spot.

If the Sox seemed interested in January, they virtually turned their backs on Strawberry in February. In fact, as spring training opened at the end of February, Strawberry found that no team was willing to sign him. Indeed, it felt like a twenty-six-team "blacklist." Friends had suggested he contact the high-profile agent Dennis Gilbert, whose client list included Bobby Bonilla, Bret Saberhagen, Barry Bonds, and John Franco. Others close to Strawberry nudged him in the direction of Baltimore-based attorney Ron Shapiro, whose ethics and track record of fair play were beyond reproach.

But Strawberry hardly seemed to be in any condition to make choices. In addition to the death of his agent, Strawberry learned in January that his mother, Ruby, was battling cancer, and a month later she died. As a result, he was so disoriented he decided he was incapable of even a simple task like choosing a new representative, saying, "I just don't know who I can trust."

As crushed as Strawberry was by Goodstein's death, he couldn't have been surprised. The agent had had a history of heart disease and was further troubled by acute diabetes. In the week preceding his death, the fifty-six-year-old Goodstein was admitted to Bellevue Hospital to treat the insufferable pain in his right leg, a result of diabetes-related circulation problems. But the agent didn't dare burden Strawberry with his troubles. Instead, he and Darryl spent Friday evening on the phone going over all twenty-six teams, trying to decide on the best fit in '96.

Incredibly, the Yankees weren't out of the running. George Steinbrenner had told aides that if Darryl were still out of a job by spring training, he would invite him to camp for yet another audition. But Darryl expressed reservations about returning to the Yankees, no doubt fearing it would appear he was crawling on his hands and knees.

"They did me wrong, that's for sure. And besides, if I went back to the Yankees, I'd only play part-time," Strawberry said. "I'm still too young for that. I still got enough talent to help some team."

That's why the Red Sox appealed to Goodstein. They were said to be offering his client $800,000, with enough incentives to make it worth Darryl's while. But the Friday-night talk Strawberry had with Goodstein would be the last time they ever spoke. On Saturday, Goodstein called Darryl's home in Rancho Mirage, only to be told by Charisse that her husband was still asleep.

"Don't wake him, honey. I'll call back a little later," Charisse recalled Goodstein saying. Within a few hours, Goodstein was pronounced dead at Bellevue. Ironically, Goodstein correctly predicted the circumstances of his death—he was stricken in his office: "I spend so much time in my office, where else am I going to die?" he said to friends one day in 1991. Friends were always an important currency to Goodstein; he had always considered himself a networking champion, a lawyer/agent with the greatest connections in New York City. But in the end, with the exception of Strawberry, Goodstein was utterly alone. He had systematically cut off each of his close friends, not calling some and picking fights with others. He had even fired his secretary two months earlier, seemingly without any provocation.

Those in Goodstein's circle theorized that his apparent personality change was related to his illnesses. "Bill was taking so many painkillers for his legs that, in effect, he became an addict," Ray Negron said. "He had to pop so many pills just to get through the day, and, when the painkillers wore off, he was slightly off, always angry, looking for a fight."

Negron had his final conversation with Goodstein in August, just as Dwight Gooden was dismissing Goodstein. For the rest of the summer, Goodstein attacked his former partner—in private, to officials at the Players Association, and in public, on sports-talk radio. Goodstein even went as far as to have Negron decertified as an agent. That's how deeply he felt Negron had betrayed him by taking on Gooden. Perhaps there was some envy, too, because Gooden breezed through the late fall and winter without money or drug or employment problems. Gooden was a Yankee and spent the months working out in peace.

But despite their distance, Negron wept openly upon hearing of Goodstein's death. "I'll only remember Bill for the good times, not the last six months," he said. "They said when they started cleaning up his office, my name was scribbled all over his legal pads. It just broke my heart."

Another lifelong friend, a Manhattan attorney named Mike Mitchell, also had a falling-out with Goodstein and never had a chance to say good-bye. "We argued about something on the phone three months earlier, and Bill just hung up on me," Mitchell said. "I didn't call him; I thought it was his place to call me first. But he never did. And then one day, Bill just died."

Staring at the casket at the Riverside Chapel on Manhattan's West Side, Mitchell thought of the lesson Goodstein's death represented. "It meant, to me, no grudge is worth taking to one's grave," he said.

In a way, Strawberry was living that same credo, dedicating the '96 season to Goodstein and his mother. "All I need is a chance to play, so I can play in his memory."

Just one more chance, one more stage to stand on, enough room for the long swing that could capture a ballpark. Just one more at-bat, because Darryl Strawberry could always make the world his own once he got to the plate.

One more chance from baseball. Strawberry wondered if that was too much to ask.

THE 1986 WORLD CHAMPION METS: THEN AND NOW

ADMINISTRATION

Frank Cashen, general manager: Retired from active involvement with the club after the 1991 season, ending a twenty-five-year career as a baseball executive. Now lives in Florida and serves as a part-time consultant.

Joe McIlvaine: vice president: Left the Mets in 1990 to become the San Diego Padres' general manager but returned to accept the general manager position with the Mets in 1993. Has quietly and systematically rebuilt the franchise after its crash in 1992.

Al Harazin: vice president: Became general manager after Cashen's retirement in 1991, gambling heavily on free agents Bobby Bonilla and Vince Coleman and trading for Eddie Murray and Bret Saberhagen. The team lost 193 games in two seasons before Harazin was relieved of his responsibilities. He resigned in 1993. Most recently served as a part-time consultant to the United Baseball League.

MANAGERS, COACHES, INSTRUCTORS, TRAINER

Davey Johnson, manager: Fired in 1990 after the Mets stumbled to a 20-22 start, ending a seven-and-a-half-year association with the club during which he was 595-417, a .588 winning percentage. Spent three years outside of baseball—blacklisted, he believes— before returning as manager of the Cincinnati Reds, where he won a Central Division crown in 1995. Hired as Orioles manager in December 1995.

Bud Harrelson, infield coach: Replaced Johnson as manager after his 1990 dismissal. Harrelson failed to make it through an entire season, as he was dismissed before the end of the '91 campaign. Club fell to 77-84, twenty and a half games out of first place. Replaced by Jeff Torborg for the '92 season. Currently works with the Mets community relations department.

Sam Perlozzo, third-base coach: Fired after the 1989 season, the casualty of a power struggle between Cashen and Johnson. Became Lou Piniella's third-base coach with the Seattle Mariners.

Bill Robinson, hitting instructor: Fired with Perlozzo in 1989 for the same reasons. Currently managing the Phillies' Double-A affiliate in Reading, Pennsylvania.

Mel Stottlemyre, pitching coach: Became the Astros' pitching coach in 1993, then agreed to a similar position with the Yankees for the 1996 season.

Steve Garland, trainer: Dismissed after the 1994 season, for reasons he said were never made clear to him. May well have been made the fall guy for Gooden's relapse. Subsequently was the victim of what appeared to be a blacklist, after revealing to *Sports Illustrated* that the Mets used amphetamines in the eighties. One Met official admitted, "Steve didn't help himself by challenging the team like that in public. The baseball community is a close-knit one, and they're easily scared by someone who they perceive as trouble." Garland was forced to collect unemployment in 1995, until finally landing a full-time position with NordicTrack.

PLAYERS

Wally Backman, second baseman: Traded to the Twins after the 1988 season, then played his next six years with the Twins, Pirates, Phillies, and Mariners. Admittedly went into hiding after being released by Seattle early in 1993, plagued by personal and financial problems. Still struggling to pay his bills in the wake of a bitter divorce. "I really didn't want to face anyone," he said. "My situation was touch-and-go for a while. I didn't know if I was going to have enough money to get by." Currently living in Washington State, where he hunts and fishes, he is planning a return to baseball as a coach someday.

Gary Carter, catcher: Retired after the 1992 season, now works color commentary for the Florida Marlins. Says, "I consider the nineteen eighty-six season one of the greatest moments of my career."

Lenny Dykstra, center fielder: Traded to the Phillies midway through the 1989 season, and has become one of the game's premier leadoff hitters. Became a Phillie legend in 1993, when he challenged State Senator Earl Baker to a fistfight at a posh Italian restaurant. Baker had complained about Dykstra's off-color language, and the outfielder got up, walked to Baker's table, and said, "I'll drop you like a bad habit, dude."

Kevin Elster, shortstop: Plagued by shoulder problems throughout his career, he played only thirteen games between 1992 and 1994. Hooked on briefly with the Yankees, then dabbled in acting, and is now attempting another comeback with the Phillies.

George Foster, outfielder: Released in August 1986, after publicly questioning the Mets' racial policies. Currently living in Connecticut, where he runs baseball instruction schools.

Ed Hearn, catcher: Part of the much-heralded trade that brought David Cone to the Mets from the Royals days before the 1987 season. Currently living in Lenexa, Kansas, he works as a motivational speaker. He is also writing a book about the 1986 season.

Danny Heep, outfielder: Moved on to the Dodgers, Red Sox, and Braves before ending his career in 1991. Whereabouts currently unknown.

Keith Hernandez, first baseman: Left the Mets via free agency after the 1989 season, signing a two-year deal with the Indians. Played a total of just forty-three games because of back injuries. Currently serves as a free-lance broadcaster and still lives in Manhattan.

Howard Johnson, third baseman: Enjoyed a five-year surge after the '86 season, during which he hit 157 home runs. Led the National League in home runs (38) and RBIs (117) in 1991. But his production dropped off dramatically after that year, and, after signing with the Rockies in 1994 and hitting just .211, he appeared to have completed his career. He hooked on briefly with the Cubs in 1995 after signing a minor-league contract with them.

Ray Knight, third baseman: Signed a free-agent contract with the Orioles immediately after the '86 season, a defection that marked the beginning of the end of the Mets' golden era. Worked for ESPN as a studio commentator until Davey Johnson's return to managing in Cincinnati, when Knight became a Reds bench coach. Succeeded Johnson as manager of the Reds for the '96 season.

Barry Lyons, catcher: Still active through '95 season, most recently with the White Sox.

Dave Magadan, first baseman: Still active through the '95 season, most recently with the Chicago Cubs.

Lee Mazzilli, infielder: Joined the '86 team after Foster was expelled. Retired after the '89 season, he now works as an investment banker and restaurateur. Also serves as commissioner of an amateur baseball league in Westchester County.

Kevin Mitchell: Left the Mets after the '86 season, traded to the Padres and then the Giants, Mariners, and Reds. Despite his reputation as a troublemaker, at least in the eyes of Met management, he won the National League Most Valuable Player Award as a Giant in 1989 after hitting 47 home runs and driving in 125 runs. Spent 1995 playing for the Chunichi Dragons in Japan after signing a $4 million, one-year contract.

Rafael Santana, shortstop: Ultimately replaced by Kevin Elster, he played with the Yankees and Indians before retiring in 1990. Now serves as a roving scout in the Dominican Republic for the Braves.

Tim Teufel, second baseman: Traded to the Padres in May 1991 and retired after the '93 season. Currently working as a financial analyst in San Diego.

Mookie Wilson, center fielder: Retired after the 1991 season after spending the last two and a half years of his career with the Blue Jays. Forever linked to the game-six miracle in the 1986 World Series, he has maintained his association with the Mets as an employee in the community relations department.

PITCHERS

Rick Aguilera, pitcher: Still active through the 1995 season, recently signing a three-year deal with the Twins, for whom he played between 1989 and 1995, interrupted by a pennant-race stint with the Red Sox in '95.

Ron Darling, pitcher: Retired midway through the '95 season with Oakland. Currently beginning a career as a sportscaster, working pre- and postgame shows with the A's.

Sid Fernandez, pitcher: Still active despite his innumerable threats to retire and return to Hawaii. Signed with the Orioles in 1994 but failed badly, going 6-10 with a 5.47 ERA before being released midway through 1995. Friends say Fernandez was miserable because the Orioles were conservative in comparison to the old Mets. "No one there listened to heavy metal," said one friend.

At Lenny Dykstra's urging, the Phillies signed Fernandez, and he promptly won six of seven starts down the stretch in '95.

Bob Ojeda, pitcher: Retired early in 1994 after a personal tragedy, the sole survivor of the 1993 spring-training boating accident that killed Indian teammates Tim Crews and Steve Olin. Ojeda spent much of the year recovering from head injuries and, in his postaccident depression, fled to Sweden by himself and considered suicide. Finally rebuilt his career, with the help of former teammate Roger McDowell, and signed with the Yankees in 1994. But a bad elbow and lack of desire to keep playing led to retirement just three weeks into the season. "I basically didn't have it in me anymore," said Ojeda, who lives with his family in Rumson, New Jersey, where he plays golf, works out, and says, "I'm looking for something to do with the rest of my life."

Jesse Orosco, pitcher: Still active, most recently with the Orioles.

Doug Sisk, pitcher: Retired after the 1991 season after playing the last two years of his career with the Braves. Worked in a sporting goods store in Washington and as a part-time scout for the Mets but incurred the wrath of many former teammates by becoming a replacement player in 1995.

Roger McDowell, pitcher: Still active, most recently signing with the Orioles for the '96 season.

ABOUT THE AUTHOR

BOB KLAPISCH, a graduate of Columbia University, has written about baseball for the *New York Post*, New York *Daily News*, *Sports Illustrated*, and *The Sporting News*. He currently covers the Yankees for *The Bergen Record* in New Jersey.